The Over-50 Guide
to
Money-Making Business Opportunities

The Over-50 Guide
to
Money-Making Business
Opportunities

Richard Michaels

PARKER PUBLISHING COMPANY, INC.
West Nyack, New York

Library of Congress Cataloging in Publication Data

Michaels, Richard
   The over-50 guide to money-making business
opportunities.

   Includes index.
   1. Small business. 2. Vocational guidance.
3. Age and employment. 4. Success. I. Title.
HD69.S6M52   658.1'1   77-26807
ISBN 0-13-646604-4

Printed in the United States of America

A Word from the Author

The dream of your lifetime—a successful business of your own—can be just weeks away from becoming a reality.

Throughout your life, how often have you yearned for the independence, prestige and financial security of a small businessman? If that has been a perpetual dream of yours, then the time has now arrived for you to watch that wish materialize.

It's a very *possible* dream. I have interviewed dozens of successful small businessmen who have established their own enterprises, and are now earning incomes larger than they ever thought possible. A few years ago, they were like you—dreaming of where they could be, but perhaps uncertain of where to begin. But they made it—and are celebrating their decision to enter the business world on their own.

You're actually more fortunate than they are. For you have in your hands a guide to succeeding in your own business that can speed you toward prosperity. If you're serious about success, you've made a wise choice to begin by reading these pages.

No matter what your age—50, 55, 60, or more—there are exciting opportunities awaiting you. This is a marvelous time to be launching your own business, and if you're willing to follow the proven advice offered in this book, your chances for success are excellent.

Perhaps you can envision yourself on opening day—swinging open the front door and waiting on your first customers. Imagine the pride you'll feel in running your own business in the community, and the respect you'll receive from your patrons and other businessmen, too.

In this book, you'll meet people like Suzanne C., whose net profits in her camera store were $31,400 in her second year of business. You'll also learn about Robin S. and Martha J., sisters who earn $27,000 annually in their plant business. You can do as well—or better.

Readers who carefully follow the systematic plan presented in this book, and who adhere to the many tips offered, will find the life of a small businessman easier than they might have thought possible. With your experience and maturity, you have important qualities that can lead to prosperity.

As you proceed through the following pages, take notes about information applicable to your own situation. Keep in mind that the upcoming years can be the most rewarding and satisfying ones of your life. It's all up to you.

Richard Michaels

Table of Contents

CHAPTER 1

Making Money in an Over-50 Small Business

America is still the greatest land of opportunity. As you read these words, millions of small businessmen are succeeding in their own enterprises, fulfilling their personal dreams of independence and affluence.

Just drive through the main business district of your community and see the establishments that have been there for two, five, ten and twenty years—and even longer. For the owners of these businesses, their determination and dedication have paid off handsomely.

Today, there are many wealthy people who made their fortunes through independent small businesses. They started with little or nothing, but found their own niche in the community with a business that filled a definite need. They were flexible, willing to adapt quickly to changing conditions, and eager to offer personalized service. They were patient, hard-working and determined to succeed—and they did.

And you can, too.

IT'S NEVER TOO LATE!

Seymour H. remembers very well how his relatives good-naturedly teased him when he told them he was opening up his own pizza franchise at the age of 59. "They all said I was too old, and that I was stupid to give up my job as a cook," he recalls.

"Well, I didn't think my age made any difference, except that I was a little more experienced in the food business than a younger man. But a lot of people try to convince you that once you reach a certain age, it's too late to try new things. It doesn't make any sense to me."

Seymour is succeeding in his pizza franchise. In fact, he now has one of the ten most lucrative restaurants that carries his franchisor's name. If he had listened to his relatives, he would probably still be cooking for someone else—and feeling frustrated doing it.

Like Seymour, a growing number of men and women of all ages are starting their own businesses. Some are doing it as an outlet for their own creative energies; others say it seems like a logical way to prepare for a secure retirement.

People are becoming increasingly aware these days of how difficult it is to accumulate a nest egg for retirement. Many have worked for 30 or 40 years for a single company. They are often happy with their working experience and anticipate that they will enjoy a comfortable retirement someday. But when those retirement years arrive, they are often a tragic and painful disappointment. So in the hope of avoiding such circumstances, many people are now leaving their "secure" jobs to establish their own businesses, aspiring to accumulate a sizable savings for retirement.

TURNING YOUR AGE INTO AN ADVANTAGE

You should never consider your age, no matter what it is, to be a handicap—because it isn't. In fact, it may turn out to be one of your biggest benefits.

Several years ago, Col. Harland Sanders, a white-haired and goateed Social Security recipient, decided to forsake his monthly government checks in order to pursue his own personal dream. At age 65, after only a few months of retirement leisure, he created the Kentucky Fried Chicken Corp.

Now the Colonel is not only retired once again, but he is a wealthy retiree. He sold his Kentucky Fried Chicken empire for $2 million cash, plus an annual retainer of $40,000.

If you're in your middle years, or even older, this may be the ideal time to launch a small business. After all, you have had several decades of experience behind you, and as the song says, "They can't take that away." No matter what you've done in your life up to this point, the knowledge you've acquired over the years will undoubtedly help you in some way in your new venture. Whether you've been a salesman or a mechanic, a waiter or a beautician, you've learned and experienced many things. And while working for someone else, the mistakes you've made have been at his expense.

HOW THE YEARS HAVE PROVIDED YOU
WITH AN ASSET

Throughout your life, you've probably also made many contacts which a younger man out of high school or college hasn't had the opportunity to accumulate yet. You may know your banker on a personal basis, and now can turn to him for the capital you might need to start your business. You may have also become acquainted with an attorney or an accountant, whom you can call upon for advice and assistance. You most likely also know at least a few successful businessmen in your community, who can relate their own experiences to you and help you to avoid some of the obstacles they encountered.

Finally, with each passing year, you should have more self-discipline, as well as an improved ability to realistically evaluate your personal assets and shortcomings—so necessary for a small businessman to prosper.

The Unusual Business Success of Robert S.

Consider the success story of Robert S., for instance. He had worked as a department store salesman for most of his adult life. But when he reached his early 50s, he decided it was time to pursue new challenges. His children were nearly grown, and he felt that he should "finally do some of the things I've been wanting to do all my life." One of those ambitions was to launch a business of his own.

For several years, Robert had been thinking about opening up a motorcycle repair shop. "My son has ridden a motorcycle since the age of fifteen," he explains. "I've been tinkering with his machine and those of his friends from the beginning."

Upon doing some research, Robert was impressed with figures indicating that there are more than 5.5 million motorcycles registered in the U.S. That's an increase of 240 per cent over 1969. Robert also discovered that there was a scarcity of motorcycle repairmen in his community. Once he had discussed his idea with his family, he decided to establish his own shop, Freeway Cycle Repairs.

After his first year in business, Robert knew he had made the right choice. His net profits were slightly under $21,000—more money than he had ever made in his life. His shop, situated about equidistant between the big Kawasaki and Yamaha sales dealerships in town, proved to be an ideal location. As of this writing, the volume of his business is continuing to expand, and his son may soon become a partner in the enterprise.

Robert is not yet a rich man, but he is living more comfortably than ever before. And his future appears even brighter, promising the security which he has longed for all his life.

WHEN TO LAUNCH YOUR BUSINESS

Just pick up any newspaper classified section and you'll see evidence of activity within the small business community. A recent issue of the *Los Angeles Times* featured ads like these among hundreds of similar ones:

Restaurant, Bar & Deli. Fantastic location. Well known for 27 years. Loyal clientele. Includes building and property.

Printing—Quick Type. 1 yr. old, great potential, growing volume. Excellent boulevard location. Illness forces sale. Terms to qualified. Will train new owners.

Book Store. Just opened 2 months ago. 1050 sq. ft. Located in a new and very rapidly growing area of La Verne. 1000s of new homes being built adjacent to center. Must sell—will take small down and monthly payments for fixtures & inventory from responsible party.

Success in these or any other establishments is dependent upon a number of factors, but certainly timing is among the most important. Obviously, you would not launch a blacksmith business these days— that is, unless you see indications that the horse and buggy are on their way back. Instead, you'll want to focus on services or products that have achieved considerable public acceptance or demand, or soon will.

The Small Business Administration as well as the U.S. Department of Commerce periodically publish reports regarding trends in the business community. So read these for ideas on the types of enterprises most likely to succeed in the upcoming months or years. Or if you already have a specific field in mind, read the appropriate trade journals to keep abreast of significant events that might affect any business decisions you'll make.

Let's assume that you're thinking about opening up your own restaurant. Well, you'll presently find some impressive statistics to support a decision in that direction. Americans are now eating away from home more than ever before. About 24 cents of each family food dollar is spent eating out, predominantly at fast-food establishments. Food service is now the third largest consumer field in the U.S. (a $70 billion industry), trailing only the retail food business and the auto industry.

What Peter B. Discovered From Business Statistics

There are currently positive indicators in other lines of business as well. Peter B. analyzed some newspaper statistics he ran across recently, and concluded that auto supply stores would be particularly lucrative enterprises in the mid- and late 1970s. He discovered that 1972 and 1973 were peak production years for U.S. auto manufacturers, and concluded that those model cars would be in dire need of new parts, probably beginning in 1976 and continuing until they were discarded.

"Inflation and tight money have forced people to buy new cars less frequently," explains Peter. "So those '72 and '73 cars that they're hanging onto are definitely going to need tune-ups and repairs for as long as they're around."

Peter was further encouraged by a survey he came across, indicating that 60.5 per cent of all car-owning households now do some auto maintenance of their own. People are replacing their own spark plugs, changing their own oil, and tuning their own engines. This do-it-yourself trend has helped turn the auto supply business into a $28 billion industry.

After his research was completed, Peter decided that an auto parts store was what he wanted to pursue. His establishment eventually opened on his 52nd birthday, and thus far, all his projections have been validated. "I'm netting about $415 a week now," he says. "And we're getting a lot of return customers. I expect things to get even better."

The do-it-yourself trend is helping other small businesses to thrive, too. Calling in a plumber or a gardener to handle home improvements or repairs is beyond the financial reach of many people now. Thus, hardware stores and other enterprises selling various types of tools and supplies are thriving. Screwdrivers, hammers and wrenches are selling very well. So are garden tools, ranging from lawn mowers to weed pullers.

The rising crime rate has influenced small business trends as well. As the number of burglaries soars above the three-million-a-year level, the sale of security devices has risen dramatically. Companies specializing in the manufacturing, sales and servicing of sophisticated burglar alarms are enjoying enormous success in the 1970s. And there's absolutely no indication of a reversal of this trend.

All that's required is a little research and imagination to decide what businesses have the best chances for success now. Even in times of economic recessions, there are enterprises that thrive because they are tuned in to people's needs. No matter what the stock market or other indicators may say at any particular time, there are always many businesses for which *now* is the best possible time to launch them.

THE 4 KEYS TO BUSINESS SUCCESS

The next chapter will help you even more in deciding on the "perfect" type of business for you. But in addition to the kind of business itself, there are certain personal qualities that can help your small business become as profitable as possible. Study these 4 Keys to Business Success. If you possess them all, you're probably on your way to a successful venture:

(1) A genuine interest in and understanding of people.   You need customers in order for your business to prosper. And to attract them, you're going to have to know who your potential customers are, what their needs are, and what they're willing to pay for particular items. Once they've left your store, you've got to attract them back as repeat customers. So you must make sure they're satisfied with your product and service. Offer them a little something extra—i.e., your bakery shop can always have an open tray of cookies on the counter, with an invitation to try one.

(2) Experience.   You should have some familiarity with the business which you're about to enter. For instance, one of the most successful flower shops in California is operated by a former nurse. However, she took the time to learn about flowers and the flower business, including ample reading and appropriate night classes at a local junior college.

(3) Self-confidence.   If you have confidence in yourself, success is on your doorstep. And there's no reason why you shouldn't be self-assured. Think back on all the positive moments in your life. If you launch your new enterprise with a vision of success, you'll realize your dreams all the quicker.

(4) Willingness to plan.   Be willing to spend as much time as is necessary to carefully devise your "game plan" for your small business. As you proceed through this book, you'll be guided through these planning stages. You'll learn how to point your business in the most advantageous direction, and how to deal with anything that might arise. Diligent advance planning will provide many dividends for your business in the upcoming years.

THE JOYS OF THE SELF-EMPLOYED

Once your new business starts to show its first profits, you'll understand how exhilarating it can be to run your own firm. And you'll discover some attractive fringe benefits that come to small businessmen:

- —The satisfaction of being known in the community as an independent businessman, with all its special status.
- —The ability to run things the way you want to, without worrying about how superiors are going to react.
- —The pride in making something that you've created work, thanks to your own ideas and energy.
- —The knowledge that there is no ceiling on your income—you can earn as much as your energy and customers will allow.
- —The contentment that you won't be forced into retirement, whether you want to retire or not, when you reach 65 or 70.

Probably few people have enjoyed the excitement of watching their own business succeed more than Doris M. She was a high school dropout, and was even twice convicted of minor shoplifting charges when she was in her teens. Throughout her adult life, she was un-employed as much as she worked, and she often had to borrow money from relatives just to feed her two daughters and herself.

But during the 1960s, Doris worked steadily as a secretary for a fashion designer. She became fascinated with women's apparel, and soon was reading every fashion magazine that was in the office.

Finally, Doris decided it was time to move out on her own. She quit her $535-a-month job, and two months later, opened a shop called the African Boutique, specializing in fashions for black women. In addition to apparel, the shop also featured authentic African items like jewelry, works of art, musical instruments and baskets.

Today Doris sees herself as a real "rags-to-riches" individual. She netted $26,512 in her third year in business—quite an improve-ment over the $535-a-month secretarial job.

DECIDING UPON YOUR OWN BUSINESS

Doris M. found her own niche in the small business world. And you can find yours.

Don't feel limited in any way, because there's simply no reason to. Whether you're rich or poor, black or white, male or female, the opportunities are limitless.

Let your imagination run rampant, and you may create a new product that could sweep the nation. That's exactly what happened in late 1975, when a young man decided that the perfect gift for the person who has everything was a Pet Rock. The novelty item consisted of simply a rock in a box and a clever brochure describing how to care for it. The Pet Rock retailed for $4, and its creator made a million dollars before the zany fad wore thin.

A more practical enterprise was created by a Texas woman, who was amazed to learn that 50 million Americans were regular viewers of TV soap operas. She decided to publish her own soap opera news-letter, which reviewed the daily shows and outlined their plots and story lines. As word of her publication spread, tens of thousands of subscription dollars flowed into her mailbox. Today, she is on her way to becoming wealthy.

TAKE THE FIRST STEP NOW

If you're not convinced yet that the opportunities for making money are there, keep reading. Throughout this book, you'll learn about the experiences of dozens of individuals who already are running their own small business. Interestingly enough, not one of the people interviewed while researching this book expressed any regrets over having joined the ranks of the self-employed. As a middle-aged garage owner said, "Everyone should try it at one time in his life. The self-satisfaction I feel is wonderful. And the money is icing on the cake."

CHAPTER 2

Selecting the Right
Money-Making Business for You

There are few things that can be more frustrating than being one of thousands of employees at a major corporation. Even if your title and your office seem impressive to others, you may suffer from a loss of individual identity in such an environment. The impersonal nature of a big corporation persuades thousands of people every year to search for new, more creative lines of work.

No wonder, then, that the successful small businessman is such an admired member of the community. He is prospering independent of the bureaucracy of huge organizations. He has preserved his identity, and is enjoying the fulfillment that comes through self-employment.

LAUNCHING A BUSINESS NOW

Ask yourself a few pertinent questions. Have your working years been as rewarding as you had hoped? Have you achieved most or all of the goals which you set for yourself years ago? Do you wish to become more independent in the years ahead?

Your answers may point you toward one of the most important decisions of your life—to go into business for yourself.

KNOW THYSELF

Before announcing to the world that your own "grand opening" is just a few weeks or months away, keep in mind that self-employment is not right for everyone. Some people work more efficiently and are better motivated in a large organization. For them, starting a small business is not advisable.

But if you're the type of individual who is comfortable being in control of a situation, and you're willing to accept full credit or blame for what occurs, then you're probably a prime candidate for launching your own enterprise. The first step, though, is to completely analyze yourself—your capabilities, your deficiencies, your talents, your shortcomings. Evaluate yourself carefully and honestly, to judge whether a small business is right for you, and if it is, what type of business it should be.

THE 7-POINT SELF-EVALUATION TEST

Are you ready for a bit of self-analysis?

First, on a separate sheet of paper, place the letters A through G down the left side of the page. Then proceed with the following self-test, selecting the description under each heading that most closely fits you. There is a score after each description, and you should place that score next to the appropriate letter on your notepaper.

Now, let's begin:

A. Initiative

I am a highly ingenious person, and am always seeking new challenges and tasks.   (4)

I am usually resourceful, and respond to many of the opportunities around me.   (3)

I perform my regular work well, without needing guidance and instruction.   (2)

I perform my regular work only after waiting for instructions.   (1)

B. Organizing Ability

I am extremely capable of setting up orderly procedures and systems.   (4)

I am an able organizer.   (3)

I have accomplished some organizational chores, but frequently I have failed to do so.   (2)

I am a consistently poor organizer.   (1)

C. Responsibility

I often seek out responsibility and enjoy accepting it. (4)

Although I only occasionally seek out responsibility, I welcome it eagerly when it is offered to me. (3)

When I assume responsibility, I find it distasteful, but I am able to tolerate it. (2)

I never accept responsibility. (1)

D. Perseverance

I pursue my goals resolutely, and am not discouraged by misfortune or obstacles. (4)

I am capable of maintaining a steady effort. (3)

I am about average in terms of my determination. (2)

I give up easily, and have often changed jobs when the situation became too difficult for me. (1)

E. Energy Level

I always seem to have limitless energy when involved with something meaningful to me, and can work hard for many, many hours. (4)

I frequently feel energetic, but it is not a constant state of being for me. (3)

I am somewhat energetic, but long hours often tire me. (2)

Whenever possible, I shun hard work because my energy level is below average. (1)

F. Decision-Making

I make decisions quickly, and they are almost always the correct ones when viewed in retrospect. (4)

I am a good decision-maker, but I usually do not like to be rushed into making up my mind. (3)

I can make decisions fast, but they are frequently the wrong ones. (2)

I don't like to decide things, because my judgment always turns out to be unwise. (1)

G. Human Relations

I get along well with everyone, and find people extremely

interesting.   (4)

I am always pleasant and gracious to everyone I meet, even if he or she is not the kind of person I'd like to be friendly with.   (3)

Others tell me that I am occasionally difficult to get along with.   (2)

In many instances, I am uncooperative, and I am frequently involved in arguments.   (1)

Now add up your point totals in all the categories. If your total score falls into the 21 to 28 point range, then you're ideal material for running a successful small business. If you land in the 15 to 20 range, enter the business world, but do so with special care. If you score under 15, then you're definitely not the type of person likely to succeed in your own enterprise.

CHOOSING A NEW LIFESTYLE

Mike R. scored well on the above test. He dropped out of the "rat race" three years ago to launch his own small business. He had been employed as an accountant for a major construction company, and although he enjoyed the work itself, he hated the pressures that accompanied it. There always seemed to be one more thing to do than he could comfortably handle, and his anxiety began taking its toll on his mind and body. He developed hypertension, and his physician cautioned him that a heart attack might not be far off unless he dramatically changed his lifestyle.

That was all the warning Mike needed. He was middle-aged—much too young to retire but wise enough to realize he'd be foolish to remain at his job. So he immediately began thinking about switching to a new line of work, and he took a vacation in order to get away to consider the possibilities.

On his trip, Mike and his wife stopped in a small town about 150 miles from their own home, and that's where and when he decided what the future held for him.

"We were inside a general store—one of these real small places that sells a little of just about everything," he recalls. "The people who ran the store were so friendly and relaxed that we began talking for quite awhile. And as we talked, I kept flashing back to my childhood, when I used to help my uncle run his own store much like that one. Those were some of the happiest times of my life."

Before the day was through, Mike decided to get back to the basics, and open up a small-town general store of his own. A month later, he found one that was for sale about 35 miles down the highway, and before the year was up, he was in business for himself.

How Mike R. Built Up His Fortune

"I worked a ten-hour day, five days a week," says Mike, who goes fishing on his off-days (Wednesdays and Sundays). "When I'm not there, the place is closed, so I don't worry about someone else running the business into the ground."

Mike's revenues in his second year were an amazing $200,000, and he hopes that figure will rise as he expands the product lines that the store offers. He is one of 26,000 general store owners in the U.S., and he is delighted with his new way of life.

"I chose the general store because it allows me to take life easier," he says. "Of course, there are headaches now, too, but not the kind that used to fray my nerves and cause my stomach to churn as an accountant. And I'm making a lot of money."

SELECTING YOUR OWN BUSINESS

Not everyone, of course, would find a general store attractive. It works for Mike R., but there may be even a better choice for you. So how do you choose the small business that's best?

First, analyze your own interests and experience. What did your education prepare you for? What are your hobbies?

Scan the "Business Opportunities" advertisements in your local newspaper. Even if the businesses currently being offered are not appealing, they will give you ideas as to the type of enterprises currently in the marketplace.

Chamber of Commerce officers in your city will probably be eager to help you with your decision, once they learn that you'd like to locate there. They know what the needs of their community are, and once you tell them where your own interests and expertise lie, they may be able to guide you into an enterprise very likely to succeed.

Check with professors at the nearby business schools and colleges. They often hear of businesses for sale that you might not learn about through other channels. Also, they have a good grasp of the economy, of new trends, and of new pending legislation that might affect certain types of firms. They are an excellent source of information and advice, and are usually quite cooperative.

The Source of Margaret L.'s Successful Business

Margaret L. credits a local business professor with helping her start her own plant shop. She was simply tired of working as a clerk in someone else's store, and thought that she knew enough about plants to start her own retail outlet.

So Margaret, an attractive divorcee, enrolled in two business classes at a nearby junior college. As the semester progressed, she became more and more convinced that she should go into business for herself selling plants. One evening, she approached her professor after class, and told him about her idea. He reacted very positively, and agreed to meet with her on a subsequent Saturday morning when he could hear about her plans in more detail.

Margaret was so encouraged that, prior to that Saturday meeting, she began putting her ideas on paper—i.e., where the business would be located, the initial financial investment required, methods of attracting customers, and ways in which the business could be expanded someday. When she met with the professor, he gave her some additional suggestions, and most importantly, referred her to a local banker who he thought would be receptive to her well-conceived proposal. Within two months, she had secured a loan from the bank, and her new business was soon underway. Today, both her plants and her business are thriving.

CHOOSING A BUSINESS THAT FULFILLS A NEED

If your new business sells an item that no one wants or needs, then even the most creative advertising campaign will not turn your enterprise into a success. So once you've decided on a small business idea that appeals to you, ask yourself if it would appeal to anyone else. Do people need the product you're selling? Do they need it more or less now then they did five years ago? And will they need it five or ten years from now?

Among the fastest growing small businesses these days are ventures like instant printing centers, indoor tennis courts, and employment offices. Because of the emergence and wide acceptance of permanent-press clothing, coin-operated dry cleaning establishments are also being launched at a record rate of nearly 2000 per year.

Your business must not only fill a need, but ideally, it should do it in a unique way. Earl Gragosian opened his first Royal Inn motel in 1965, and the chain quickly spread across the country. While other motel chains were suffering financially, his was flourishing. The key to his success was his emphasis on luxury—from the majestically designed rooms and the antique furniture to the deep-pile carpeting and the full-wall murals. Some rooms had their own fully stocked bars and fireplaces. The nightly rates were high, but Gragosian was offering travelers plushness that no other motel chain could match.

There will probably always be a market for luxury, but don't forget that most consumers are even more interested in bargains. A relatively new franchise called Tred II took note of the current interest in tennis, and began resoling tennis shoes. In 1975, it resoled 250,000 pairs; in 1976, that figure doubled. As well as resoling (for $12.95), Tred II will also insert new insoles and arches, and restore the original shoe color. Customers either drop off their worn-out shoes at one of 600 tennis centers or sporting goods stores that serve as pickup points, or they mail them to a central location.

How Louis J. Met the Needs of a Market

Another recently launched business—the rental of guard dogs—is also filling a distinct need. Louis J. had always had pets throughout his life, particularly dogs. He relied on his German shepherd to keep burglars away from his own house. So when he read about a thriving business in New York that rented dogs for security purposes, it was a natural step for him to launch a similar business of his own.

Louis purchased several German shepherds, obedience-trained

them and then attack-trained them. He had no trouble finding customers once the word of his new business spread.

"Every evening, as my customers are closing up their stores and factories, I drop off a dog at each of their places," he says. "No one in his right mind is going to break into a place with a big sign warning of a dangerous dog inside. One time somebody did, and the dog nearly tore him to pieces."

Louis has about as much business and as many dogs as he can handle (19 dogs and an $85,000-a-year gross). He feels his type of business has enormous potential for others who have both the ability to train dogs and the facilities (i.e., a kennel) to house them. Do you have these qualities?

ANALYZING THE COMPETITION

In order to succeed in any business, you must be aware of the competition and know as much as possible about them. The best time to begin this investigation is when your own business is in the planning stages.

Let's assume that you're interested in starting a men's clothing store, but there is already one about three blocks from where you want to locate. How much do you know about this competitor? Is his business successful, or is it doing poorly, and why? If the store is doing well, how can you make your shop a little different? Should you specialize in sportswear, and forget the sale of business suits altogether? If your competitor is doing a good job of filling the need for business suits, you may not fare well trying to compete with him.

How Rudy C. Analyzed His Competition

Rudy C. capitalized on his own ability to analyze the competition. All his life, he has been interested in physical fitness, and has always maintained himself in excellent condition. When he was a teenager, he was a lifeguard, and then he went to college as a physical education major. He subsequently coached in junior high school. When he reached his late 50s, he decided to retire.

But Rudy soon discovered that his disposition would not allow him to retire and do nothing. He eventually decided to open up his own gym, catering to businessmen interested in keeping themselves physically fit. His enterprise was well into the planning stages when he began analyzing the competition. He knew about the franchised gymnasium a few blocks away, and was prepared to do battle with it. But when he found out about a new, well-financed gymnasium being constructed on the roof of the city's tallest office skyscraper, he decided to re-examine his own chances for success.

After weighing every factor, Rudy decided to shift gears. His gymnasium would not now cater to businessmen, but rather to children ranging in age from five to fifteen. It would be an after-school meeting place where boys could learn tumbling, calisthenics, jogging, boxing, and the basics of weightlifting.

"Things **have** worked out really well," says Rudy. "After years of teaching, I'm used to working with kids anyway. This is really an extension of what I've been doing all my life, but it's different enough so that it seems brand new. I charge the kids a monthly membership fee, and it works out to be only slightly more than what it would cost them to join the YMCA. I'm making more money than I did teaching, and have the satisfaction of running the entire show myself."

4 STEPS TO JUDGING THE COMPETITION

In summary, you'll have a pretty clear indication of who your competition is and what your own chances of success against them are by answering the following four questions. If your answers are all "yes," then the competition may be too tough. In that case, consider dropping your idea, and select another type of business with a better opportunity to succeed.

(1) Are there other stores selling essentially the same merchandise as you in the area?

(2) Are they well-advertised, well-known stores?

(3) Do you consider them to be more aggressive in their operations than you would be?

(4) Are their parking facilities better than yours?

WHERE SHOULD YOU LOCATE?

Most small businessmen, particularly those in their middle-age, decide to start their new enterprises right in their own hometown.

After all, credit is easier to get there, because bankers probably know them. They already have friends who not only might become customers, but also provide valuable word-of-mouth publicity. And on a personal level, once a person is in mid-life, he often isn't eager to move to a new city, leaving all his acquaintances behind.

However, within one's own city, particularly a major metropolitan center, there can be quite a difference between locating your business downtown or in the suburbs, in one neighborhood instead of another, or on the east side of the bridge as opposed to the west.

When Kurt B. Mayer and Sidney Goldstein conducted a study for the Small Business Administration titled "The First Two Years: Problems of Small Firm Growth and Survival," they uncovered some interesting facts. They discovered that the choice of a business location was too often based on factors like what buildings were vacant and how close they were to the owner's home. No attempt was made by many businessmen to gauge the potential that the establishment would have in a particular site. Some ignored factors like declining population, and new highways that would significantly reduce traffic through the business center. The competition was also often disregarded completely.

In contrast, the wise small businessman should carefully search for a location which will supply him, first and foremost, with the customers he needs. For instance, a record store proprietor might decide to locate adjacent to a college, where many young people congregate. However, the owner of a furniture store might want to establish his business near some new housing developments in town.

For assistance in determining the local population distribution, contact the Chamber of Commerce. The Chamber will provide you with information on community characteristics and income levels. The regional office of the U.S. Department of Commerce can provide even more detailed population breakdowns, available in its census tract maps. If there is no Department of Commerce office near you, the same maps may be available at the city or county planning departments, or in some business libraries.

The U.S. Bureau of the Census has compiled other kinds of statistics, but some just as interesting and helpful. Its figures indicate the surrounding population required to support a particular kind of store, dependent on how widespread its appeal is. For instance, the universal need for a grocery store makes it possible for it to survive on a considerably smaller population than a hardware store. Likewise, a gas station has a better chance of doing well in a small community than does a cigar store.

Below are the national averages of the population required for common types of retail establishments:

Restaurant	840 people
Grocery store	910
Gas station	920
Bar	1,790
Drugstore	3,700
Furniture store	5,980
Women's apparel	6,240
Hardware store	7,320
Jewelry store	8,400
TV store	8,720
Florist	8,860
Small appliance store	9,560
Retail bakery	10,150
Sporting goods store	12,400
Department store	34,580
Cigar store	35,770

As well as situating your business adjacent to the type and numbers of consumers you're interested in, you should also study the following about a potential location:

— The number of people who pass by—on foot and in cars— during a typical day.
— The hours during which the traffic is the heaviest.
— The types of businesses nearby.
— The availability of public transportation near your store.

If your business is the kind that depends heavily on "drop-in" customers, you should locate it on a busy street. Corner sites are considered ideal, because of their greater visibility from several directions.

Neighboring stores can also influence the number of customers you'll attract. Research has shown that certain types of stores do better when located near other specific types. For instance, men's and women's clothing stores usually do well when they are near department stores. Restaurants and candy stores often thrive when they are adjacent to theaters. And paint stores, home furnishing establishments, and furniture stores have a good chance of success when they are in close proximity to each other.

Just as there are certain desirable neighbors, there are some undesirable ones as well. There is normally little or no foot traffic around garages, bars, hospitals, heavy industry and mortuaries—so avoid them.

How Ralph B. Chose a Liquor Store Site

Most liquor stores are stocked with essentially the same merchandise, sold for approximately the same price. So location is a key factor when a new liquor store is opened, since it may be the only advantage that one store has over another. Thus, when Ralph B. was preparing to open up his own liquor establishment, he spent several weeks searching for just the right site.

Ralph's first stop was the Chamber of Commerce, which gave him statistics on income levels in various sections of the city. He was attracted immediately to the higher-income areas, densely populated with professionals.

Then Ralph took a drive through the vicinity, trying to determine whether the area really needed another liquor store. He not only visited the liquor stores in the neighborhood, but also markets and department stores that also sold liquor.

Because most liquor store customers live within a one- or two-mile radius of the establishment, Ralph narrowed his choices down to two areas where there was just one other liquor store in the immediate vicinity.

He then jumped into his car once again—this time to search for a store for lease within those vicinities. He narrowed his choices down to a site within a small shopping center, and a vacant building across the street from a department store. He eventually decided upon the shopping center site, because of its neighborhood "flavor" and the parking lot that would be available for his customers.

4 RULES FOR NAMING YOUR BUSINESS

Whenever a new business is founded, unless it is part of a franchising operation, a name must be chosen for it. A name can be an important part of the new enterprise, grabbing the attention of passers-by and, hopefully, leaving an indelible mark on their minds.

There are four rules to follow in selecting an effective name:

(1) Pick a name that's simple and easy to remember. "Manchivsky's Diner" is not nearly as preferable as a catchy name like "Blazing Salads."

(2) Use a name which tells the customer what service or product you're offering. A name like "Smith and Sons" gives no such information, while "Smith's Stationery Supplies" does.

(3) Avoid overused words in the name, like "famous," "quality," "discount," or "bargain."

(4) Take care to ensure that you've not chosen a name already in use. You can register your trade name with the United States Patent Office, which will give you the right to its use for 20 years, with one renewal of another 20 years allowed. The Patent Office in Washington, D.C. will provide you with further information and an application.

GETTING THE TRAINING YOU NEED

Common sense tells you that you should know something about the business which you are entering. For instance, it would be unwise for an auto mechanic to open up a party store, unless he entered the enterprise with a partner who knew the field well.

Some aspiring small businessmen are willing to spend a year or two becoming acquainted with an unfamiliar field before starting their own establishments. Thomas K., who had been a cosmetic salesman for many years, quit his job to work in a bookstore for 12 months, in anticipation of opening up his own book shop. Once he had learned how to buy, order, receive, record, display and sell books, he launched his own business.

If you're interested in starting your own plant store or nursery, you can take courses in ornamental horticulture and botany at your local adult school. You should learn the names of plants, their grow ing requirements, and methods of propagation before opening your doors for the first time. Knowledge of caring for sick plants is also a necessity.

In certain types of businesses, state laws require that you have specific training. For instance, if you want to operate your own dry cleaning plant in California, you must take 360 hours of training at an approved trade school, and then pass a comprehensive test. Only if you've worked 12 months for a licensed professional cleaner can you bypass the classroom prerequisite.

All states require that a beauty salon manager be a licensed cosmetologist and hairdresser. However, the requirements for securing that license vary considerably from state to state.

SETTING YOUR PROFIT-MAKING GOAL

As you proceed through the planning stages of your new business, it's not too early to set a money-making goal for yourself. How much do you want to earn the first year? The second year? The fifth? The tenth?

Write down the figures you have in mind. By putting them on paper, they will seem all that much more realistic to you.

Remember that few people ever become millionaires. But your small business can allow you to live very comfortably, with profits of $20,000, $30,000, $40,000, $50,000 a year and up. These are realistic goals.

CHAPTER 3

10 Proven Ideas for
Money-Making Business Success

There is immense variety in the small business world. Just mention almost any product or service that the consumer is interested in, and small businessmen probably play a part in meeting that consumer need.

So much diversity exists in the marketplace today that everyone desiring to enter the small business community can certainly find some enterprise suitable for him or her. And once that business is launched, a blend of care, perseverance and a willingness to work can result in both personal satisfaction and financial reward.

This chapter will focus on 10 specific types of small businesses which could prove to be your own springboard to success. They are typical of the enterprises which you can launch. However, they are not necessarily those that are the most likely to succeed. Literally hundreds of other fields can be entered into, depending on your own interests. But these that are described in the ensuing pages should stimulate and inspire your thinking, and also acquaint you with how others have succeeded in the business world. And, who knows, one of them may be just right for you.

AN INDEPENDENT CAMERA SHOP

Did you know that the typical American household adds 91 snapshots to its family photo album every year? In a community of 25,000 families, that's nearly 2.3 million photos that have to be processed and printed annually. Add to that the cameras that are sold to shoot them with, and the necessary film, flashbulbs and accessories that are bought, and a camera specialty store seems quite attractive. Particularly in the 1970s, with simple instant-loading cameras proliferating through millions of households, the photography business has never been better.

But before moving any further, keep in mind that a camera shop is not for everyone. If you don't know the difference between an f/16 or an f/8 camera setting, or if you're unsure when to use Ektrachrome film as opposed to Kodachrome, then think about some other type of business. The field of photography can't be learned overnight, even by diligently reading the latest brochures that Eastman Kodak has to offer. And when customers pose questions or ask for advice, the successful camera shop owner should know the answers without any hesitation.

How Suzanne C. Launched Her Camera Shop

Suzanne C. had been taking photographs for many years before she launched her own camera shop in 1974. Photography was only a hobby, but over the years, she had set up a darkroom in her own home. She owned three cameras and six interchangeable lenses, and she had read every book she possibly could find on the subject of photography. All this was done in her leisure time, quite apart from her job as a registered nurse.

When Suzanne finally decided to start her own camera store, she certainly had a thorough understanding of photography and photographic goods. Although she was aware that several drugstores and variety stores in the neighborhood were already selling and processing film, she believed that she could outdo them with better service. She was right.

Suzanne's net profit in her second year of business was $31,400. Needless to say, she doesn't regret for a moment having given up the nursing profession for a career in a small business.

When you initially stock your camera store, you'll probably obtain your inventory from three to five major wholesalers. If possible, visit the offices of these suppliers, and meet as many salesmen and sales managers as you can. Although camera wholesalers will not usually sell on consignment, they often make exceptions and concessions with new stores. A personal visit can help show the wholesaler your enthusiasm and interest in his product, and encourage him to work with rather than against you.

Also make arrangements in advance with a photofinishing firm to process the film that customers leave at your store. Do this early to give the company enough time to prepare work envelopes and provide you with any displays you may want. Keep in mind that more customers will come into your store to have film processed than for any other reason.

In the ensuing months or years, after your business is well-established, you can consider doing your own film processing right in the store. Suzanne, for instance, now has a black-and-white custom lab in her shop, where she develops and prints all black-and-white film left with her. (She still sends color film, which is more complex and expensive to process, to an outside film company for developing.)

As well as processing photos for everyday customers, Suzanne has a few business clients, too, including three local advertising and public relations agencies, which often order 200 or more 8×10 prints at a time, to send out to the national press.

Of course, printing requires a good deal of expertise. And even though Suzanne still has her own home darkroom, she nevertheless feels more comfortable hiring an experienced lab technician to work in the darkroom in her store. This technician was trained in photography in the U.S. Army, and now works fulltime for her. He can make a good 8×10 print in under two minutes, which Suzanne then sells for from 75 cents to $1.75 each, depending on the size of the order.

"I'm having great fun being in business for myself," says Suzanne. "Photography used to be my hobby; now I'm making a great living at it. I'm in an ideal situation."

THE T-SHIRT BUSINESS

Have you noticed that young people don't wear plain T-shirts anymore? Instead, their shirts are imprinted with every conceivable image—from photos of their favorite rock music celebrity or sports star to ads for popular products.

Yes, "billboard" T-shirts are the hottest clothing item since blue jeans became a commonplace piece of apparel for the young in the early 1970s. And the investment required to cash in on the T-shirt business is minimal. All you need is some blank T-shirts, a variety of "heat transfer" designs, and an iron-on hot press that can cost as little as $300 to $350.

If there is already a shop or two that sells these novelty T-shirts in your community, you shouldn't necessarily forsake the entire idea. Many moderate-sized communities have three or four such shops—all of which are doing quite well. The key is selecting the proper location for your store.

How Morris J. Tripled His Sales Volume

Morris J. opened up his T-shirt shop in 1975, just two blocks from one of the city's largest high schools. His store is next door to a large record shop, where teenagers always congregate, and down the street from a penny arcade that also attracts young people. So his location seems ideal.

For less than $1000, he obtained all he needed to get his enterprise started, including the press, an assortment of 150 heat-transfer designs, 500 T-shirts in various sizes and colors, and the first month's rent on the store he was occupying.

Business was good those first few months for Morris, but one evening while driving home from work, he came upon an idea that soon tripled his sales volume.

"I was driving by the high school, and it occurred to me that there was a potential huge market right on campus itself," recalls Morris. "Every school has dozens of clubs—like the Ski Club, the Mountainclimbing Club, the Speech Club, and so on. I decided to make contact with the presidents of these clubs on all the junior high and high school campuses in town, and try to interest them and their members in buying some custom-made T-shirts with the name of their club on it."

Morris' idea has paid off handsomely. Using a transfer letter set that he purchased, he was able to design attractive custom-made T-shirts saying whatever a particular club requested. Some weeks, he would sell more than 100 T-shirts just to club members, in addition to his regular over-the-counter sales. And since T-shirts tend to wear out after several months of use, repeat customers have become a major part of his business.

Morris' success is well documented in his yearly profit statements. His net profits were nearly $24,000 in his third year in business—an incredible figure considering that his T-shirts sell for an average of less than $4.00 each.

If the T-shirt business interests you, contact some of the companies that sell the equipment you'll need to get started. For instance, iron-on presses are marketed by the Hobard Manufacturing Co. of Ft. Lauderdale, Fla., and the Insta-Lettering Machine Co. of Los Angeles. The heat-transfer decals are available from Roach Studios of Worthington, Ohio, and Holoubek Studios of Butler, Wisc. And blank T-shirts can be bought at wholesale from a variety of firms, including the Union Underwear Co. and BVD Knitwear, Inc., both of New York City.

BICYCLE SHOPS

For a time in the 1950s and early 1960s, bicycles seemed to be going the way of the horse and buggy. With two or more cars in every garage, families were relying on bicycles less and less for mobility. The kids were the only ones who still rode bikes, but even they were pedaling less frequently because of the rising rate of accidents between bicycles and cars.

But times have changed, and bicycles have gained new respectability. So if you're looking for a profitable business to enter, don't ignore the possibilities contained in those two-wheelers.

Since the ecology movement of the late 1960s, and the inflated gasoline prices of the early 1970s, bicycle sales have been booming. Many adults are now pedaling to work, in newly created bicycle lanes that some cities have created for safety. Family weekend outings now frequently entail bicycling to the park, the beach or the museum.

Charles M. currently has one of the most successful bicycle shops in the country. He enjoys his job—and his entire life, for that matter—which is something he couldn't say even just five years ago.

It wasn't too far back in time that Charles was an assembly-line worker at an automobile manufacturing plant. He disliked the work, but he stuck with it for more than two decades, feeling that he wasn't qualified for any other kind of employment. He was a high school dropout, and believed he should be grateful for the job he had, considering his lack of education.

The Experience That Dramatically Changed Charles M's Life

But Charles' outlook on life changed dramatically almost overnight. And it took a frightening disease—cancer—to motivate him to reevaluate how he was living. Doctors found that Charles had a malignant tumor on his leg that was growing in size. After surgery and radiation treatments, the physicians cautiously pronounced him "cured." But the experience changed his life dramatically.

"I decided I had to start doing something more meaningful with my life," recalls Charles. "Life is too short to waste any of it on a job that you hate."

Six months later, Charles celebrated the grand opening of Village Bicycles, featuring sales, rentals, and repairs. Now during Christmas season and the summer months, Charles has to hire additional help because business is so good. In the week before Christmas in 1975, he sold more than 100 bikes—his best week ever. And with most bikes selling for from $70 to $200 each, and with a markup averaging nearly 100 per cent on the wholesale price, he is quickly accumulating a nestegg that will make possible an early retirement.

TRAVEL AGENCY

Probably the most fortunate of small businessmen are those who can earn their living in a field that also serves as their hobby. For instance, ask the typical travel agent what he likes to do on his vacations, and he'll probably say "travel."

Most travel agents have done a lot of traveling in their lives. In fact, nothing could prepare them any better for their jobs. It would be foolish to presume that you could be a competent travel agent if you've never ventured outside the city limits of the town in which you were born. After all, how can an agent accurately describe or recommend attractions on the other side of the country when he's never been there?

A travel agency is a glamorous business, and with more people traveling now than at any time in history, the potential for success has never been greater.

However, keep in mind that a travel agency involves a lot of hard work. The competition is keen, particularly now that most airlines maintain their own toll-free 24-hour-a-day reservation services. Still, as travel becomes more expensive, people are looking for bargains, which is where the knowledgeable agent can provide his greatest service. Package tours, which the agent can provide at considerable savings to the consumer, have become particularly attractive as inflation continues. For this reason, agents have never experienced a more lucrative time than now.

How Travel Agents Earn Their Money

A travel agent earns his money through commissions (which usually average 5 to 10 per cent) from airlines, resorts, and hotels which participate in the discount tour packages he creates. So if an agent puts together, say, a 50-person tour, with bookings totaling $45,000, he will receive $3150 in commissions if his service charge averages seven per cent.

An individual who operates a travel agency must be certified by the IATC (International Air Travel Association) and the ATC (Air Traffic Conference of America) in order to sell airline tickets. Likewise, a travel agent should also be certified by the Trans-Atlantic Passenger Steamship Conference, the Trans-Pacific Passenger Conference, and Rail Travel Promotion Agency.

To obtain these certifications, a person must demonstrate his reliability, and show that he is able to plan trips and sell transportation tickets. If you've traveled a lot in your life, you probably already have most of the expertise you'll need to make your travel agency a money-making enterprise.

GIFT STORES

Think of all the occasions during the year that you buy gifts. Birthdays, weddings, anniversaries, graduations, housewarmings, Christmas, Easter, Mother's Day, Father's Day and Valentine's Day—

they all send consumers scurrying into the marketplace to buy presents of various sizes and prices.

Gift stores alone account for nearly $4 billion a year in sales. And if you enter the field, you can share in the enormous profits possible with such a shop.

Probably the two biggest factors that determine success or failure in a gift shop is location and a personal touch. If you live in a tourist town, is there room for a gift shop adjacent to the zoo, the amusement park, or the beach resort?

Also, what can you offer in terms of individuality that a department store can't? Can you stock unusual items, or can you offer special bargains at various peak sales periods? For instance, during the Christmas season, when most stores have a sales volume that is 300 per cent higher than at any other time of the year, can you keep the fad items in stock—whether they be the latest in china or the newest Raquel Welch poster?

How Dorothy W. Increased Her Qualifications to Operate a Gift Shop

Dorothy W. felt particularly qualified to run a gift shop. She is the mother of six and the grandmother of another six, and, as she says, "It seems like I've never stopped buying gifts for someone or other."

Of course, although Dorothy has probably bought hundreds of gifts in dozens of gift shops over the years, she is also wise enough to realize that one needs other qualities as well to make a gift shop a success. So she spent more than nine months talking to other gift shop owners, gift item wholesalers, Chamber of Commerce representatives, and even potential customers—seeking advice on how best to launch her own shop.

Finally, Dorothy decided to take over an existing store—one adjacent to the city's biggest tourist attraction. She saw the shop listed for sale in a gift trade publication, as well as the local newspaper, being sold by a couple who had decided to retire after successfully running the shop for 17 years. She bought the entire operation, including inventory, fixtures, and office supplies. The store not only sells souvenirs directed at tourists, but general gift items that appeal to the townspeople as well.

Dorothy has made a success of her enterprise. She had been a housewife for more than 25 years before launching her own small business. The only work experience that she previously had was as a salesclerk in a dress shop before she got married.

"This is just as exciting, in its own way, as raising a family," she says. "I'm really doing something stimulating, and bringing in a very attractive income (about $18,000 annually at last report). My husband is still working, so we're able to put almost all of my income into the bank, saving it for our retirement. He'll be able to retire earlier now because of the money I'm making and saving."

PET SHOPS

Consider these facts emerging from the current American scene.

— One out of every two families in the U.S. has at least one pet.
— Americans spend more money on pet food than baby food.
— A small pet shop can be started with an investment of as little as $1000 to $3000.

Despite such encouraging information, hundreds of cities throughout the U.S. have fewer pet shops than they need. And the reason is that pets have become incredibly popular in recent years with people who never before thought they could own one—in particular, apartment dwellers who now have everything from cats to tropical fish to parakeets.

So if you like animals, there are excellent prospects for success in a pet shop, particularly one located in the suburbs of a metropolitan area where pet ownership is now flourishing. Experts say that a pet shop should be located in a community with a minimum population of 20,000 to achieve prosperity. An even larger population will increase the chances for success.

The animals that you sell can be obtained from a variety of sources and wholesalers. One of the most common approaches used by new pet shop owners is to attend dog, cat and other animal shows, to meet and talk to breeders. Arrangements can frequently be made for the shop owner to sell the animals on a commission basis, getting 30 to 60 per cent of the sale price. This eliminates the necessity for the new shop owner to invest sizable amounts of money in the animals he will stock.

Also, don't stock only the most common animals, like dogs, cats or parakeets. It would be wise to regularly read the pet trade journals, as well as pay attention to the requests of your customers. For instance, any pet store that doesn't stock tropical fish these days is passing up a significant sales item. According to one trade journal, collecting tropical fish is the second largest hobby in the U.S., and is not far behind photography, which is in first place.

Also, once your pet shop is doing well, and you have some extra capital to invest, you should consider stocking some of the more exotic pets, which people are now buying as much for status as anything else. These include monkeys, snakes, raccoons, ocelots and margays.

How to Enhance the Appeal of a Pet Shop

You can also enhance the appeal of your shop by adding a pet grooming service to it. This service will not only bring more people into the store, but will probably also add to your goodwill. Of course, make sure that you or the groomer you hire knows what he's doing. You can't learn proper dog or cat grooming from a book—it must be learned by doing, either at a vocational school or from someone who is already proficient in the field. Although poodle owners will be your biggest customers, you'll eventually deal with many breeds of dogs and cats, and to be an expert, you'll have to learn specific grooming techniques that apply to particular breeds.

Most successful pet store owners find that evening hours are essential, so many are open from 10 a.m. to 9 p.m., six days a week, although some only stay open late on Mondays and Fridays. Many close on Sundays, finding that Sunday is not nearly as important to sales volume as are evening hours during the week.

TV REPAIR SERVICE

When Stan S. was just out of high school, television was barely coming into its own. Stan recalls his parents' first TV set—an eight-inch model that attracted all the neighbors who wanted to see what this new-fangled invention was all about.

Stan still has that old set, and today it's on display in the store-front window of his TV repair shop—West Side TV Service. Stan opened up his shop a week after his 48th birthday, and now, three years later, he has two technicians working for him just to keep up with the business that comes his way.

Throughout his life, Stan held a variety of jobs—everything from cab driving to gardening. He loved working with his hands, and prided himself in the fact that he never had to call a plumber to do any work in the house. Instead, he was able to fix every leaky faucet and clogged pipe that ever occurred.

How Stan S. Stumbled into a Profitable Business

When Stan enrolled in a TV repair class at the local junior college, it was as much out of curiosity as anything else. He was primarily interested in learning how to fix his own TV, which seemed to be in the repair shop almost as much as it was in his living room.

But by the time the course was completed, Stan was already making plans to launch a TV repair shop. He already had a station wagon, which he now uses when making house calls. He invested in some tools and testing equipment, bought some parts, and opened up his shop. He's taking home nearly $500 a week now, and sees the opportunities for expansion as almost endless.

A TV repair business, despite the competition, can flourish these days in the right location and with the proper promotion. Millions of TV sets are bought each year, and families with two or more TVs are no longer rare. Every set needs some repair work during its lifetime, so TV repairing is a business in which potential customers can include nearly every family in your community.

When you open up your business, be prepared to do some advertising—in the Yellow Pages and in the local newspaper—just to let people know that you exist and where you're located. The ad needn't be elaborate, simply saying something like:

TONY'S TV REPAIRS
1775 McDougall Rd.
276-8195
Expert service at fair prices.
In your home or at the shop.
Free estimates.

If you offer quality work, word-of-mouth will soon make such ads unnecessary.

SECURITY-DEVICE SHOP

Skyrocketing crime is one of the tragic realities of modern American life. In many cities, people can no longer walk the streets safely at night. Almost everywhere, homeowners are adding extra locks and alarm devices to their doors and windows—usually for their own peace of mind, but sometimes also at the insistence of the company that insures their house and possessions.

Consequently, there is now an enormous market for security devices—not only for homes, but for businesses as well. And although they exist in limited numbers, shops specializing in selling security devices are expected to be some of the most successful small businesses in the upcoming decade.

Sophisticated alarm systems wholesale for a wide range of prices, but a typical one can be purchased for $250. You can then turn around and sell it to a customer for twice that amount. Sales of a dozen of these devices a week, which is not unusual, can bring you an impressive income in no time at all.

Although most security device shops work out of traditional storefront offices, one Los Angeles man also has a mobile van, filled with his equipment, which he parks in shopping centers and takes to swap meets. He demonstrates his equipment to passers-by who might never otherwise think of investigating the possibility of buying an alarm device for their home.

APPAREL STORES

Some stores will never lose their potential for acquiring customers. A grocery store is certainly one of them, because people will always have to eat. But close behind are apparel stores, because barring a major social revolution, people will also always be wearing clothes.

Certainly, competition is stiff in the clothing industry. But every year, there are new shops that are founded that do amazingly well. You can prosper if you choose your location carefully, follow the demands of your customers, and offer personalized service.

If you'd like to start your own clothing store, but are unfamiliar with the business, you'd be wise to get a job for a year or so as a salesperson in a clothing shop. Accumulate as much know-how as you can about the industry, and be thinking about the kind of store you'd feel most comfortable owning—one that features men's apparel, women's, children's or a wide selection for both sexes and all ages. Or possibly your store can specialize only in clothes for large or small-sized men or women, or feature only leather goods or western wear or bridal gowns.

Probably the biggest mistake that owners of new apparel shops make is to buy stock according to their personal tastes. Remember that customers are hardly ever interested in buying what you like, but rather what they like. It takes some time to judge the type of customers you're attracting and the clothing that they like. But if you tune into their tastes rather than your own, you'll be well on your way to running a successful—and very profitable—apparel store.

SEWING AND NEEDLECRAFT SHOP

Not everyone buys their clothes in stores. A growing number of people—in an attempt to reduce family clothing budgets—is making some clothing at home, via sewing, knitting, crocheting, needlepoint and embroidery.

Young women in particular have become home stitchers in large numbers, with the market expected to increase in the coming years. Not only can the needle arts save consumers money, but they are a very satisfying outlet for self-expression.

Shops which sell sewing and needlecraft goods are now doing very well, and can look forward to a boom period in the next few years. If you already know something about fabrics and yarn, you're one step ahead of many of your competitors.

How Agnes N. Was Forced into a Profitable Activity

That was the case with Agnes N. Her husband died suddenly of a heart attack, and although life insurance took care of the immediate needs of herself and her family, she knew she'd eventually have to find some means of income. Starting her own business seemed like a monumental task, and yet, it still would not be much more difficult than trying to find a job working for someone else after being out of the workforce for 18 years.

Agnes' friends encouraged her to go into business for herself with a sewing and needlecraft shop. She had always been talented at sewing, long before it became fashionable to be so. Thus, it would be a natural way for her to earn a living.

At first, Agnes was a bit shaky, but once she finally decided to try it, she plunged in with all her energy. It didn't take long until her shop was open and had a loyal clientele. When business got good, she hired a salesgirl, and Agnes began spending most of her time teaching morning and evening sewing classes. She charges a nominal fee for the classes ($20 to $40 per series), but her students also end up buying their class material from her store, and afterward many become regular customers.

"I suppose any new business carries some risks," says Agnes today. "But I just decided that I was going to succeed—no matter how much energy it took.

"I'm not rich yet, but I might be someday. Being forced to go out on my own was frightening, but it was one of the best things that ever happened to me."

CHAPTER 4

The Low-Cost Way of
Getting Rich After 50

Every business—even the largest corporations in America—starts out small. Just as with your own enterprise, most businesses are launched when one man or one woman has an idea and some initiative. The most successful undertakings in the U.S. begin on this small scale, and grow into the immense companies that they become.

No matter what your dreams are for your own new business, you'll need money to get it off the ground. Your ability to save or borrow this money is every bit as important as selecting the proper location for your new enterprise, or hiring the best employees for it.

How much money must you have? Actually, probably a lot less than you might think. You don't necessarily have to spend a lot of money to make a lot. This is particularly true with service-oriented businesses, like real estate agencies, advertising and public relations agencies, consulting services and employment agencies.

FOUNDING AN EMPLOYMENT AGENCY

When Louise R. started her employment agency, her initial investment was just slightly more than $1100, and that was without cutting any corners. Her major expenses were leasing an office, installing telephones, mailing out letters and cards to employers, and placing an ad in the Yellow Pages.

As Louise has learned, a small investment can reap attractive financial rewards. She was an executive secretary before starting her own business, earning a maximum of $960 a month. Now she earns a net of $2000 a month, after paying the salaries of her three employees. And if the business continues to grow, she anticipates hiring a fourth person soon.

"I think the 1970s and 1980s will be a very good time for employment agencies," comments Louise. "There's a lot of competition for good jobs, and employers are willing to pay a fee to agencies like mine to screen the hundreds of applicants who may apply for a single position."

CALCULATING YOUR INVESTMENT

Every businessman, of course, would like to keep his initial investment in his new enterprise to a minimum. That is particularly true of many individuals in the over-50 age bracket. After all, more than someone in his 20s, a middle-aged person is thinking ahead to his retirement, and would like to leave as much of his nestegg in a bank account as possible.

To help you estimate the size of the investment you'll need for any particular new business, write the numbers one through four on a separate sheet of paper, and then research the cost of each of the following items:

1. Opening Expenses. How much will it cost to put the business in order for opening day? This would include obtaining the proper licenses and bonds, paying for any needed legal and accounting services, doing any remodeling on the store, and paying utility deposits. Use your phone to call appropriate people and offices to determine exactly what these expenses will be.

2. Running Expenses. What will your continuing costs be, such as rent, utilities, insurance, salaries, stationery, postage, printing and deliveries? Again, make a few phone calls, and determine rents in the neighborhood in which you'd like to locate. The phone can also help you ascertain precise costs for the other items, like advertising and stationery.

3. Furniture, Machinery, Automobiles/Trucks. These can all be purchased used. Or if you're very dextrous, you can build some of the tables and shelves yourself. Try using the phone here, too, to get quotes on current prices for these products—both new and used.

4. Stock. How much will it cost you to stock your store with sales items? Naturally, you want your store to have as much variety as possible in terms of the products you sell. But if you have to pay cash for everything in your store, you'll probably run short of money long before your grand opening. So shop around for suppliers who will offer you a long-term payment schedule. Even a 30 or 60 day grace period after receiving the bill can give you a month or two to get the business rolling. Even better, try to obtain as much of your stock as possible on consignment, in which case you'll only have to pay for items that you sell.

WHERE WILL THE MONEY COME FROM?

Once you've estimated the initial capital requirements of your new business, then a source for it will have to be found. And in most cases, the best source is you.

Can your own savings account provide at least part of the money? Mel R. asked himself that same question when he began his own instant print shop. Actually, Mel was fortunate enough to have the $12,000 needed to launch the business. But he felt uncomfortable withdrawing that much money from his savings account to finance his endeavor.

"It literally would have taken all my savings to get the business off the ground," recalls Mel. "And nobody likes to completely deplete his savings. You always want a little to fall back on in case of an illness or other emergency."

How Mel R. Found Additional Sources of Money

So Mel resolved that he would put up $8400 of the necessary $12,000, and borrow the remainder. And he turned to his friends and relatives for the additional funds.

"My friends and family had helped me through some really tough times over the years, particularly when I had been out of work for almost 11 months on one occasion," he says. "So I borrowed $1200 each from three different people. I have them to thank for the success my print shop has had."

Mel's shop is located less than half a mile from the biggest high-rise office buildings in town. And when many of the city's major businesses need some quick printing, he is the one they turn to. In his third year in business, Mel's earnings exceed $30,000.

SHOULD YOU BORROW FROM FRIENDS?

If you're going to borrow from family and friends, the loan should be made as formal and businesslike as possible. Your lawyer and/or accountant should prepare a legal note, specifying how the loan will be repaid, and at what interest rate.

Mel, for instance, decided to repay his loan within a year's time to each lender, in nine equal monthly payments, beginning four months after the money was loaned. So each person he borrowed from received the following note, which Mel's accountant prepared for him:

For consideration received, Mel R. promises to pay Charles N., Ralph M., and Dorothy Y. the sum of One Thousand Two Hundred Dollars ($1200.00) each, with interest accruing at 6½ per cent per annum. Payments to be made per the following schedule—

Payment #	Payment Date	Portion of Payment Applied to Principal	Interest	Total Payment
1	1-1-75	$ 113.19	$26.00	$ 139.19
2	2-1-75	133.30	5.89	139.19
3	3-1-75	134.02	5.17	139.19
4	4-1-75	134.75	4.44	139.19
5	5-1-75	135.48	3.71	139.19
6	6-1-75	136.21	2.98	139.19
7	7-1-75	136.95	2.24	139.19
8	8-1-75	137.69	1.50	139.19
9	9-1-75	138.41	.75	139.16
		$1200.00	$52.68	$1252.68

Incidentally, agree with your lenders in advance that the money they are loaning you in no way entitles them to a voice in how the business will be run. Let them know beforehand that you are the decision-maker, so as to avoid quarrels that may develop later.

BORROWING FROM A BANK

Although family and friends can be a convenient source of necessary capital, most people nevertheless end up borrowing from a bank. At first, you might feel uneasy walking into a bank and asking for a loan of several hundred or thousand dollars. But it really need not be an intimidating experience at all, particularly if you're well-prepared before ever sitting down with the loan officer.

First, keep in mind that it takes about one month for a bank to approve a loan. Thus, don't wait until the last minute to begin the loan application process. Start preparing for your trip to the bank well in advance of ever entering its doors.

THE 5 CRITERIA FOR SUCCESSFUL BORROWING

Before a bank will loan you or anyone else money, it will make every attempt to examine your character and your professionalism in starting your new business. Essentially, the institution will use five criteria in determining whether or not to grant you the loan:

1. What type of individual are you? Do you seem sincere, and do you have the devotion to your new business that will be necessary for it to succeed?

2. What are your plans for the money you will borrow? Have you carefully thought out how each dollar will be spent? How much will be appropriated for buying fixed assets? How much for seasonal inventory?

3. What are your plans for repaying the loan? Do you anticipate that it can be repaid in six months, one year, or longer? How realistic are your projections? Have you taken out other loans in the past that you have repaid promptly according to the agreed-upon schedule? Is your general credit rating good, or do you have some bad marks against you regarding misuse of loans or credit cards?

4. Have you been realistic enough in your loan application to provide for unexpected developments? Have you anticipated problems that could arise, and have you prepared for them by having a little extra financial cushion for unforeseen expenses?

5. What does the future appear to be for a business like yours? For instance, if you're going to open your own record store, is the

general outlook for this type of business good? Does the record industry itself anticipate growth in the upcoming years? Also, what are the
prospects for your own particular store? Have you chosen a good
location for it, or are you planning to open it across the street from
the largest record store in the city? Have you already made arrangements with record distributors so your shop will be well-stocked with
the products that your customers will want?

IMPRESSING YOUR BANKER

Phil M. knew that launching his furniture store was dependent
on getting a bank loan. Without it, he would have to forget about his
lifelong dream of starting his own business.

So Phil decided not only to be well-prepared for his meeting
with the bank's loan office, but also to make as formal a presentation
as possible to the bank.

Thus, Phil took out pencil and paper, and put in writing the
following information, which he knew the bank would find of interest:

1. A description of his new business, including the reasons he
   plans to start it, and the products it will sell.
2. A statement of why the loan is necessary for his business to
   open and prosper.
3. An analysis of how the loan will be repaid, and in what length
   of time.
4. A description of his competitors, and why he believes his
   business will do well against them.
5. Research into the general outlook for his type of enterprise in
   the upcoming years, including reports made by banks, investment houses, and business periodicals.
6. A projection of his expected sales and profits for the first
   years of business.
7. A complete financial statement of his personal net worth,
   composed of a list of all assets and liabilities. His assets included
   cash in his checking and savings accounts, the current market
   value of his stocks and bonds, the cash value in his life insur-

ance policies, the market value of his house, the trade-in value of his automobile, and the market value of his home furnishings (furniture, appliances) and personal possessions (clothing, jewelry, etc.). His liabilities included the unpaid mortgage on his house, the balance on his automobile loan, and the outstanding bills on his charge cards.

Equipped with this information, Phil made an excellent impression upon the loan officer. It was obvious that Phil had thought out his plans for his new business well, and the bank loaned him the full amount of money he had requested.

"The loan officer told me that the written material I had prepared really helped sway the bank to my side," recalls Phil. "Also, I was helped in other ways by putting everything down on paper. It caused me to do some hard thinking about my business, and the direction I wanted it to go."

FINDING A BANK

If your city is like most others, there are dozens of banks you can choose from when applying for a loan. So deciding which one to do business with can be a tough decision.

First of all, find one that has a "venture capital" department, which specializes in lending money to new businesses. These departments are designed to grant loans to first-time businessmen who may have never borrowed money for any reason before.

Also, shop around for a bank that definitely wants your business. Some bankers seem more intent on working against you than with you. They may not appear at all accommodating to any particular problems you may have, and may convey the impression of being more interested in working with big corporations than with small businessmen. These kinds of banks should be avoided.

However, there are banks and bankers who consider small businessmen to be valuable customers. They will not only be very receptive to your loan application, but they will go out of their way to offer valuable advice on how best to make your business succeed. Go from bank to bank until you find one that seems to be on your side.

NEGOTIATING THE LOAN

Albert G. went to four different banks before he came upon one that he wanted to conduct business with. He and two partners needed $20,000 to start a small plastics manufacturing business. They got the loan, and have parlayed that investment into an enterprise that has incredible sales of nearly $1 million a year.

"When we went in for the loan," recalls Albert, "we certainly had no status in the community. So we didn't have much leverage from that standpoint. But we were determined to arrange the best possible loan we could."

What Albert and his partners did—and what you should do as well—was approach the loan officer with as much confidence as possible. They didn't let the aura of the bank frighten them, and instead went in with an attitude that the bank could not turn them down. As far as they were concerned, it was just a matter of agreeing to the terms of the deal.

"We obviously wanted the money very badly," says Albert. "But we tried our best not to act as if we were desperate. We found that our attitude prompted the loan officer to 'give' a little on the terms of the loan. We convinced him to knock off one-half of a percentage point from the original interest rate, which ended up saving us quite a bit of money."

Remember that you should never agree to terms that you can't live with. If the monthly payments are going to be higher than you can manage, then find another bank that will offer you a more reasonable repayment schedule. Once you have signed the loan contract, you are bound by its provisions, so ask questions and request changes before putting your signature on the dotted line.

PREPARING YOUR COLLATERAL

With some bank loans, the only security that will be required is your signature. However, in other cases, you might be asked to provide some additional assurance that the loan will be repaid, particularly if there is a flaw or two in your credit history.

Don't panic if collateral is insisted upon, because the bank will often be flexible in the type it will accept. You might be able to use the warehouse inventory of your new business as collateral. Some banks will also accept the pledge of your accounts receivable, or installment notes receivable.

Of course, more traditional kinds of collateral can also be used. Life insurance policies are always good collateral. So are marketable stocks and bonds, although because of factors like possible market declines, banks will usually lend no more than 75 per cent of the market value of the stocks, and 90 per cent of the value of federal or municipal bonds.

Real estate is another acceptable form of collateral, and one that appeals to loan officers. Banks will request complete details about the property, including its location, its physical condition, its foreclosure value, and the level of insurance protecting the property.

A final type of collateral of which you should be aware—but one to be used only as a last resort—is to have an endorser or a guarantor sign your loan contract. Essentially, the endorser is an individual who will sign a note to bolster your own credit. If you fail to pay back your loan for any reason, the endorser is liable to make the note good.

By asking a friend or relative to serve as an endorser, you are asking him for the use of not only his good name, but also for a willingness to back you up if you fail to make your payments. So do this only when no other type of collateral is available.

SBA Supports Andy B.'s "Sun Business"

The friends of Andy B. used to call him "a mad scientist." He always seemed to be tinkering with something in his garage, creating all types of devices that appeared to be a decade or two ahead of their times. His inventiveness was quite out of character for a man who made his living as a butcher in a local supermarket.

For years, Andy had been developing a solar energy system, which eventually became so sophisticated that he began using it to heat water for his house.

"I realized that I was on to something here," recalls Andy. "If the solar unit that I had put together could be mass-produced, I felt it would have sales potential. It seems to me that this country is eventually going to have to turn to solar energy on an immense scale."

Maybe Andy had convinced himself of the potential of solar

energy, but it seemed that no banker in town agreed with him. As one loan officer after another told him, solar energy is just too risky a venture at this time. They all rejected his loan application.

Although discouraged, Andy was not quite ready to abandon his dream. One morning, he showed up at the local office of the U.S. Small Business Administration. He asked for a loan application, which he filled out and submitted. Five weeks later, the SBA granted him a loan.

Today, Andy's first units are on the marketplace. They are retailing for about $850, and Andy makes $250 profit on each one. If his personal projections pan out on the future popularity of solar energy, don't be surprised if Andy is well on his way to being a millionaire within 10 years.

IS THE SBA FOR YOU?

The Small Business Administration may be your own key to success in your enterprise. Rather than bore you with the history and purpose of this government agency (if you're interested, the local SBA field office can fill you in) let it suffice to say that it is one of the most significant sources of loans for small businessmen.

But before the SBA will provide you with financial assistance, it will request some evidence that you've attempted to obtain a loan elsewhere. So be prepared to show the agency that you've been rejected for loans by at least two banks.

In evaluating your loan application, the SBA will use many of the same criteria that a bank would. Your character will be scrutinized, as well as your credit record and your net worth.

Don't feel that you must have an elaborate business in order to get an SBA loan. True, in recent years, the SBA has awarded loans of as much as $650,000 and more to large endeavors. But other SBA loans of as little as $1000 have been made to small undertakings.

About two-thirds of the loans made by the SBA involve participation by a commercial bank. The SBA will encourage a bank to loan you the money by guaranteeing up to 90 per cent of the loan. When no bank can be found that will make such a guaranteed loan, the SBA will then often make a direct loan itself, usually up to a maximum of $100,000.

Incidentally, once you've received an SBA loan, the agency will offer you whatever counseling and guidance you may need to ensure that your business prospers. The SBA feels that a lendee who fails is a blemish on its own reputation. So it will do whatever it can to see that you succeed. Many recipients of SBA loans are now the wealthiest small businessmen in the country.

CHAPTER 5

Making Your Fortune in Franchising After 50

Whenever a new Jack-in-the-Box or Holiday Inn opens up in your city, do you find yourself wishing you were involved in the enterprise? Do the status and the glamour of a nationally known company appeal to you, and seem like a very attractive way of entering the business world?

Well, you're not alone. Many other people have had similar thoughts in recent years, and have acted upon those feelings. Consequently, franchising has flourished in the past decade, and shows no signs of losing its momentum.

Essentially, franchising is a way to go into business *for* yourself but not *by* yourself. A franchise exists when a large company gives you the right to sell, distribute or market its product, using its name and selling techniques.

At its best, this type of business arrangement is attractive for both the parent company and the operator of the individual sales outlet. The franchising company is able to establish a large chain of outlets to sell its product, for a relatively small capital outlay on its own part. And each individual franchisee is operating his own business with the advantage of being aided by the experienced franchiser.

With each passing year, your chances of succeeding in franchising are improving. Studies on the subject verify that an increasing number of franchises are experiencing prosperity these days, and those with financial problems are becoming more scarce.

There are probably already dozens or even hundreds of franchise success stories in your city. Just glance at the local outlets of McDonald's, Kentucky Fried Chicken, or Aamco Automatic Transmissions. It's not a mere coincidence that these franchises are rarely lacking customers. Patrons are obviously being satisfied, and a few franchisees are actually becoming millionaires in the process.

IS FRANCHISING FOR YOU?

Successful owner-operators come from all walks of life. If you're thinking of investing in a fast-food franchise, for instance, keep in mind that you don't necessarily need background in the restaurant business (although it would obviously help). Each parent company has its own training program, which is designed to turn a novice into an expert by the time of the grand opening.

McDonald's, which is the most successful franchise operation in history, selects its owner-operators from a variety of backgrounds. Those now operating McDonald's restaurants include former government officials, office workers, dentists, engineers, military men, salesmen, and business executives. According to one McDonald's spokesman, previous restaurant experience might even be a handicap, since the McDonald's system of operation is so different from all others.

3 QUALITIES FOR FRANCHISING SUCCESS

Before you read any further, pause a moment to evaluate your own chances for success in a franchise. It takes a special type of person to adapt to the requirements imposed by a parent company. In the final analysis, a franchisee is not entirely his own boss. True, he runs most of the show himself, but still must accept some guidelines from the company.

Ask yourself the following three questions. If you can answer "yes" to all of them, your future as a franchised small businessman is probably bright.

1. Can you work well under supervision? Most parent companies have a set of regulations which you must follow, and an area advisor who will drop by occasionally to check how your business is doing. If you don't feel you can tolerate any restraints put on your business, then a franchise is not your best choice.

2. Do you have the business qualifications necessary to run a franchised business? Although you don't necessarily need prior experience in the particular field in which your franchise is involved, you should have other, more general qualities. For instance, will you be able to handle the added paperwork that is part of the franchised

operation? And if not, will you properly delegate this responsibility to a competent accountant?

3. Can you honestly be enthusiastic about the franchised product you will be selling? If you really aren't interested in the line of goods, then don't bother with the enterprise. It's better to open up your own small business selling a product you like, rather than launching a franchised, nationally known business promoting products that you loathe. Your chances of success are many times better in a business you believe in than in one you don't.

HOW MUCH WILL IT COST?

The cost of starting a franchise business is not always cheap. It will usually cost you more to open, say, a franchised fast-food restaurant than one that you launch on your own. At McDonald's, the franchise fee and the cost of equipment for one restaurant totals about $160,000—and that's before the first hamburger ever comes off the grill.

Of course, although a big-name hamburger franchise might cost $160,000, there are other types of franchises on sound financial footing that sell for much less. One survey indicates that the cash investment required for small franchises is as little as $2000. About half of all franchises demand less than $15,000 capital. The careful investor can find a franchise that he can afford.

How Ralph P. Shopped for a Franchise

Take, for instance, the case of Ralph P. Like thousands of other people, he had fantasized about opening up his own McDonald's restaurant. But the pricetag on such a venture put it way out of his reach.

Still, that didn't keep Ralph away from the franchise restaurant business completely. He began investigating other fast-food franchises—Lum's, Pizza Hut, Arby's Roast Beef, Jack-in-the-Box, Kentucky Fried Chicken, Weiner King, and others—searching for a more realistic opportunity. He finally decided upon Golden Skillet, a growing franchise that sells chicken, shrimp, fish and chips, and other dishes.

"It cost me $7500 to get the initial franchise license," recalls Ralph. "That was much more reasonable for what I was getting than anything else I had heard about. And business is great. Next year, I'm hoping for a sales volume of close to $300,000."

Golden Skillet franchisees are required to attend a one-week training session in Richmond, Va. Many other franchises have similar mandatory training programs.

CASHING IN ON THE FRANCHISE PHENOMENON

Tens of thousands of Americans are earning very comfortable livings in the franchise business, and most of them have launched their endeavors in the past decade. But even though franchises have boomed only in recent years, don't feel that you're getting involved in a new and untested phenomenon. Franchising is a well-established system of marketing goods, dating back to the post-Civil War period when the Singer Sewing Machine Company became the first firm ever to franchise dealers.

Today, franchised businesses include almost every type you can imagine—including auto repair shops, print shops, drug stores, car washes, furniture stores, travel services and employment agencies.

FRANCHISING'S ADVANTAGES AND DISADVANTAGES

Larry M. had been a small businessman for 26 years when he switched gears and started his own trailer rental business under a franchise. Prior to that, he had operated a small stationery store, which provided him with a comfortable living. "But frankly," he says, "I was looking for a change. I wanted something which would allow me to be outdoors for part of each day. I had heard a lot about franchising, and decided to investigate the pros and the cons."

Larry did some research into the type of business he would start, finally deciding upon a trailer rental enterprise. Then he analyzed whether to launch the business himself, or to buy a franchise.

By the time his research was completed, Larry had a list of arguments on each side of the franchise issue. His list of pros and cons, which appear below, can serve as your own guide of the general advantages and disadvantages of any franchised business.

ADVANTAGES:

1. The parent company gives each franchisee substantial guidance and assistance on a variety of important business matters—everything from preparing and marketing the product, to creating goodwill and effective promotion, to designing signs and fixtures. The established name and reputation of the franchise also are part of the package, as are nationally advertised products or services.
2. Many franchisors provide their operators with help in selecting a favorable site, designing and equipping the structure once it is found, and establishing proper accounting procedures.
3. Most parent companies furnish training to their new operators—i.e., how to cook hamburgers, or how to replace mufflers. Once the franchise is open, management assistance is offered on an ongoing basis.
4. If you're in need of a loan to raise the necessary capital to obtain a franchise, a bank may look more favorably upon you with a franchisor standing behind you. Some franchisors will even co-sign your bank note, thus guaranteeing your loan if you should be unable to keep up with the payments.
5. Fewer franchised businesses fail than do businesses that individuals launch on their own. One reason is that many parent companies will do their utmost to keep their franchises from collapsing. Bankruptcies are considered bad, not only from the point of view of profits, but also as they affect the "image" of the franchisor. McDonald's, for instance, claims that not even one of its franchised restaurants has ever lost money.

DISADVANTAGES:

1. The costs of a franchised business are usually higher than for a business being started from scratch. As well as paying an initial charge, the franchisee continues to pay the parent company a regular royalty fee, which can range anywhere from 2 to 15 percent of the total gross sales.
2. A franchisee must usually abide by all of the policies of the parent company—not only those that he feels benefit him, but

also those he believes hurt him. If, for instance, the chain produces many products, each franchisee is expected to sell all of them, even those that may not be profitable for him.

3. Depending on the degree of control that a particular parent company demands, some franchisees sense that they are only fulfilling the role of "manager" instead of "small businessman." You should inquire in advance how much control you're going to have. If it seems either too much or too little (depending on your own desires), then look for another franchisor.

FINDING A FRANCHISE FOR YOU

There are many ways to determine which parent companies are currently looking for franchisees. Probably the Sunday classified section of a major newspaper is a good place to start.

The following ads appeared in a recent Sunday newspaper, and are typical of the kind you're likely to find:

> **Owning a National Graphics store can be better than having a rich uncle.** For an initial investment of $15,000 (secured) you can own your own business and serve all other businesses with a vital need . . . "while-U-wait" quality printing. We provide a ready-to-operate business which includes four (4) weeks training, advertising and marketing program, computerized accounting systems, group insurance plans and continuous support.

> **Anthony's Pizza is a growing company with over 200** locations that recognizes continued growth is best realized when the franchisor has something of value to offer a potential franchisee . . . What we offer is a franchise package including: site selection criteria and critique, format design, assistance in equipment purchasing, complete management training program, operations format, marketing and financial assistance. Licenses are now available. Let's talk.

Home Protection is quite possibly the most exciting innovation in the home resale market in over 100 years. Provides an inspection and guarantee backed by an insurance policy which covers the major structural and mechanical systems of a home—protects home buyers, sellers, lenders and realtors, and makes for a quicker sale and a safer buy. Can you qualify for an area franchise?

THE FRANCHISE SHOWS

Millie C. knew she wanted to start her own business, but wavered when it came to selecting the precise type of business she was really interested in. At times, she thought about a gift shop. But a fried chicken franchise also seemed attractive. And so did a doughnut shop.

For months, Millie contemplated her future, but seemed no closer to a decision as time passed by. Sometimes, her own indecisiveness made her think that she'd remain a housewife for the rest of her life. Then she heard about a franchisor exhibition being held in her city, in which parent companies were going to present their business packages to potential franchisees. It seemed like an excellent opportunity to be formally introduced to many different business opportunities at once, and to meet the representatives of various companies.

How the Franchise Show Helped Millie P.

Millie went to the two-day show with as much enthusiasm as anyone else who was there that weekend. She picked up hefty handfuls of literature on her first day there, and took them home to read. By the second day, she had narrowed her choices down to two particular franchises—an ice cream parlor and a doughnut shop. She spent her entire Sunday talking to representatives from the two companies. By day's end, she had decided upon the ice cream parlor, and plans began for her to launch the business. Today, she operates the franchise with incredible success, particularly during the summer months when ice cream sales skyrocket.

If you live in a major city, there is probably a franchisor exhibition held there once or twice a year. If you write a letter to the International Franchise Association (7315 Wisconsin Ave., Suite 600W, Washington, D.C. 20014), it will be able to inform you on the date and location of the next franchisor show nearest you.

TIPS ON SURVIVING THE EXHIBITION

Your major goal in attending a franchisor's exhibition should be to obtain information and have your questions answered. However, when you're doing your exploring, keep the following tips in mind to get the most out of the show.

1. Ask specific questions and demand specific answers. Don't let yourself be swayed by superfluous distractions like shiny new equipment or bikini-clad girls.
2. Don't be influenced by a fast-talking salesman who attempts to get your signature on a franchise contract immediately. Don't fall for the suggestion that you "leave a small deposit before you go home." A legitimate franchisor will not use high-pressure techniques if he's truly interested in entering into a long-term agreement advantageous to both parties.
3. Beware of unscrupulous franchisors who use plants or shills to try to convince you that their franchise is worth investing in. These shills may be introduced as "a franchisee who opened his business a year ago and already is a millionaire." Talk to such a person with caution; he may not be who he says he is.

OTHER SOURCES OF FRANCHISE INFORMATION

Even if no franchisor exhibition is scheduled for your city soon, there are other sources of franchising information of which you should avail yourself. Check, for instance, the publications in your library that pertain exclusively to franchising. For instance, *National Franchise Reports* is a monthly newsletter that describes new franchises and provides information on the industry in general. *Modern Franchis-*

ing is published bimonthly, and is a magazine with news and advertisements about the subject.

Also, read trade publications that are directly related to the kind of business you're contemplating. For instance, if you're interested in an automobile-related business, read copies of periodicals like *Auto Merchandising News* or *Automotive News*. If a pet shop sounds appealing, keep abreast of current copies of *Pet Age* or *The Pet Dealer*. Ask your librarian to help you find the appropriate trade journals for your particular interests.

Other important sources of information are annual directories in franchising. One of them, *A Franchise Directory*, is issued by International Franchise Opportunities. The other, *The Franchise Annual*, is published by the trade journal, *National Franchise Reports*.

You might also drop a note to Sales and Distribution, U.S. Department of Commerce, Washington, D.C. 20230, and request a free copy of *Franchise Company Data*. This book lists the various types of franchising outlets, the particular parent companies that conduct each of these businesses, and how much capital is required to get started. The book will also tell you how long each company has been in business, how many franchises it currently has operating, and the type of training and financial assistance that is offered (if any).

IS THE FEE WORTH IT?

Franklin K. operates a franchise electronics shop in the neighborhood he has lived in for all of his 58 years. He had been a civil service employee most of his life, and became a small businessman three years ago. In his third year in business, he took home $31,000. He is delighted with his current situation, but he cringes when he thinks back to how close he came to not starting the business at all.

"The franchise fee turned me off at first," says Franklin. "I just hated to dip into my bank account, which wasn't that big to begin with anyway.

"But I sat down and figured out what I was getting for the fee. First, I was able to use the franchisor's name and his image. The fee also covered the costs of all the training I received, including my room and board when I was at the training school, and even a small salary during the training. After I weighed everything, I would still be paying more than if I had opened up a business all on my own, but not that much more. I don't regret it at all now."

Like almost all other franchisees, Franklin is still paying money to the parent company, but now in the form of royalties, which average four per cent of his gross sales. He also pays the franchisor an additional 1.4 per cent of his gross sales, which is spent on national advertising. But even with these continuing expenses, he is earning a very comfortable living.

"It's worth it," says Franklin. "People know the store's name because of the advertising, and I could never really afford the ads if I were on my own."

BEING AWARE OF RIP-OFFS

Ask any consumer advocate if all franchise stories have happy endings, and it's likely that you'll hear a resounding chorus of "noes" in reply. Although success stories are now common in franchising, they are not universal. In fact, franchising weathered some incredibly difficult times in the late 1960s, when rip-offs within the industry were rampant. Tighter restrictions have eliminated most of these problems, but the potential franchisee still has to be wary of dishonest parent companies.

Of course, when you're conducting business with a company with a national reputation, you can be relatively certain that you won't be cheated or deceived in the agreement. But judging the small and relatively new franchisors is more difficult.

Whenever you're talking with representatives of a franchise, keep the following points in mind to help you avoid the fly-by-nighters:

— Avoid any franchisor who promises a get-rich-quick deal. No business has its success guaranteed. Instead, look for the franchisor who provides you with attractive but realistic projections as to the future of your proposed business. If you're promised overnight wealth and a mansion in the most expensive neighborhood in town, don't waste your time talking any further.

— Make sure you understand fully the depth of the training programs being offered to you. In many cases, the training is superb. But with some franchisors, the "training" consists of nothing more than a few pages of mimeographed reading material.

— Don't let a celebrity name sway you. Rarely does the celebrity participate to any significant degree—i.e., he's not going to spend all of his Saturday afternoons at your store bringing in customers and signing autographs. More important is the strength and soundness of the operation itself.

THE FAST-FOOD FRANCHISE

Several times in this chapter, I've made mention of one type of fast-food franchise or another. And for good reason. Restaurants are among the most popular of all franchises, and many do well simply because of their national reputations.

If you're already thinking about opening a small restaurant, you should probably at least consider a franchised operation. It is becoming increasingly difficult for the independent restauranteur selling similar food to compete with the franchise down the street. The name value of places like McDonald's or Kentucky Fried Chicken is enormous, and is reflected in the sales figures of the various outlets.

The major fast-food franchisors simply won't let failure happen. They promote their products with multi-million dollar advertising campaigns, they oversee the operation of their outlets carefully, they conduct an endless number of market studies, and they seem one step ahead of the lawmakers when it comes to adapting to state and federal legislation that affects them.

How an Established "Name" Helped Porter R.

Consider the case of Porter R., for example. He had run a restaurant when he was in his mid-20s, which enjoyed reasonable success. But he sold it after eight years, and went to work for someone else as a bartender. Then at the age of 48, he and two friends joined forces to buy a fast-food franchise, one with a well-known name.

The competition was very stiff, but their restaurant did fantastically well from the day it opened. "The name alone drew people in from everywhere," said Porter. "We really didn't have to build goodwill. We bought it when we invested in the franchise."

The future of franchised food outlets looks particularly bright. In the early 1950s, only a few pennies out of the typical family food dollar was spent on meals away from home. By 1980, it will probably hover at about 50 cents of every dollar.

HARD WORK PAYS OFF

Determination is as much a key to success in franchising as with any other type of small business. For three decades, Stephen K. had been nurturing a dream of opening up his own auto repair shop. It seemed that every time that dream came close to fruition, some serious setback occurred—including a recurring illness that victimized his daughter and drained both his emotions and his bank account.

Still, Stephen persevered. He finally approached a muffler shop franchisor, hoping to launch his own outlet. He had done his homework well, and was able to present a very impressive picture of himself as a responsible husband, father and member of the community. The company agreed that he was the right man for one of its franchises.

"I started the muffler shop at an age when I really didn't feel I wanted to spend 5 or 10 years trying to build up a reputation in the community," says Stephen. "In the automobile business, the public is apprehensive. They're extremely suspicious that they're going to be cheated at every turn. People don't want to put their car in just anyone's hands, so the nationally known name of the muffler company meant something to them. It carried credibility with it, and made it easier for me to attract customers from the start."

ANALYZING THE FUTURE

Profits at most types of franchised outlets increased substantially in the mid-1970s, and according to the U.S. Department of Commerce, that trend will continue for the foreseeable future. According to Commerce Department spokesmen, the fastest-growing franchises in the near future will include: (1) business services, like real estate sales and rentals, employment agencies, printing and duplicating shops, and tax preparation; (2) recreational services like exercise clubs; and (3) training services like day-care centers and nursery schools, and secretarial establishments.

No matter what type of business you finally decide upon, there are three additional points which you should carefully heed before ever signing your name to a franchise contract:

1. Check as carefully as possible the financial standing of the franchisor. Ask your own bank to help you check on its financial condition. If it is inadequately bankrolled, it may not be able to fulfill its promises of financial assistance and expansion. Also, is the franchisor a one-man company or a corporation with an experienced management?

2. Make an effort to talk to other franchisees already operating businesses in the chain that you are interested in. Phone them, or visit them at random. What is their advice? Do they have complaints or grievances? Also, show these franchisees the projected income figures that the parent company has given you, and ask whether they are realistic.

3. Don't rely on the franchisor's lawyer to represent your interests. Instead, have your own lawyer read and study carefully any contract you are asked to sign. Preferably, your lawyer should have franchise experience. Does the contract seem to offer the franchisor more benefits than it offers you, or does it reflect a feeling of mutual benefit? And does the contract ask you to do anything which may be illegal or unwise in your city or state?

CHAPTER 6

Buying an Existing
Money-Making Business

How Raymond C. Reduced His Risk

Raymond C. simply did not want to take any chances when entering the business community for the first time. Frankly, he knew very well that for a small business to be a big money-maker, every possible variable should be in its favor.

Raymond felt that one of the surest ways to success would be to buy an existing business with a proven track record. He would feel a lot more confident about becoming an independent businessman if he were taking over a store that was already doing very well.

"I had just had major surgery six months earlier, so I knew I couldn't handle anything too strenuous," says Raymond. "In fact, the reason I never went back to my old job as a long-distance trucker was that it was just becoming too much for me."

One morning, Raymond noticed a small two-line classified ad in the local newspaper:

Photocopy business for sale.
Reasonably priced. Call 285-7614.

He was on the phone immediately, and later that day, he was visiting the current owner. The business was being sold because the owner was getting divorced and planned to move to another city. The photocopy center made copies for five cents each, and as its accounting books showed, business was good. The small enterprise was located across the street from a local college, and students used the facility to make photocopies of term papers and a variety of other school assignments. Businesses in the area also found the five cents-per-copy rate very reasonable, and regularly used the service.

"I bought the business for very little money," says Raymond.

"And there was no dropoff at all in customers when I took over. In fact, business picked up quite a bit when I began selling school supplies in the shop. Students started buying paper and pencils from me because I was selling them at a slightly lower price than the college bookstore was.

"I work five days a week, and it"s really not hard work at all. It s a one-man business, and my profits are about $80 a day. That's about $20,000 a year."

Raymond's success story is encouraging for everyone who has contemplated buying an existing business. Although there are laws against fraud and misrepresentation, all of us are still fearful of buying a business that is sick or dying. True, an existing enterprise offers great opportunities for the new small businessman. But choosing the right one demands as much careful investigation and study as does launching a business from scratch.

4 REASONS TO BUY AN ESTABLISHED BUSINESS

There are certain advantages to buying an existing enterprise. The following points will help you clarify in your own mind what they are, and assist you in deciding if an established business is the proper choice for you.

1. The owner who created the business has attended to organizing it and training the current employees.
2. The store is already stocked with both merchandise and equipment.
3. A clientele has probably already been built up by the previous owner. If you continue to provide these customers with good products and service, they will probably continue to frequent your establishment, despite the change in ownership.
4. You will have a proven location for your business. Unlike when a business is started from scratch, you won't have to guess whether a location is good or not; the accounting books will indicate very clearly whether customers are attracted to the store where it is currently situated.

Of course, along with these concrete advantages, you are also assuming certain potential perils that are unique to buying an existing business. For instance, if the business has been mismanaged in the past, you may be taking over the previous owner's headaches. In addition, you will inherit *all* of his inventory, even those items which you no longer plan to sell. Also, as well as inheriting whatever goodwill the business has accumulated, you'll also acquire any negative reputation that has been created in the past. There is also the risk of being misled into paying too much for the business, due to either your own inaccurate appraisal, or misrepresentation by the seller.

FINDING AN EXISTING BUSINESS

If you consider yourself typical, then it will probably take you between six months and a year to find a going business that you'll finally end up buying. Before that, you'll probably come across some other enterprises along the way that are interesting, but upon weighing the pros and the cons, you'll decide against them. If you find the business that you want to buy a week after you start looking, consider yourself extremely unusual. Likewise, if it takes you two or three years to discover it, you are once again out of the ordinary.

When you reach the one-year point, and you still haven't found "the perfect venture," then you should probably take a breather and analyze your situation. Do you really want a business, or are you only playing games with yourself as well as the sellers who you have been talking to? Keep in mind that a prosperous businessman has to be decisive, and if you find yourself unable to make up your mind about one business after another, then maybe you should re-evaluate whether you really want to enter the business world.

STUDYING EXISTING BUSINESSES

James H. had decided that a going enterprise was the best way for him to become part of the business community. But he felt insecure trying to evaluate what a particular business had to offer. He had never run his own enterprise before, so he was unsure of what to look for in a business up for sale. If the right deal came along, would he even be able to recognize it?

Finally, James decided to ask for some advice from his local banker. Together, they put together a series of questions that James then used to determine whether a particular small business was suited for him.

You can use these same questions in your own search for the ideal existing business. They are questions which any seller should be willing to answer.

— Why is the present owner selling the business? Is it being sold because it's losing money? Or are there personal reasons?

— What do the records indicate? Are profits increasing steadily? What sales trends have occurred in the business over the past few years?

— Do any liens exist against the business?

— Are any back taxes owed that you will have to assume as the new owner?

— Is the inventory all timely, fresh and usable, or is some of it obsolete or deteriorating? If some of it will have to be disposed of, is the seller willing to assume the loss?

— Are all the equipment and fixtures in good working order, or will they have to be repaired or replaced?

— Are the suppliers of the business convinced that the enterprise is being well-run. Ask the present owner for the names of his suppliers, and contact them by phone.

— Has the store built up any goodwill by becoming involved in the community in any positive way? For instance, is it active in local charitable events, or does it belong to the Better Business Bureau or the Chamber of Commerce?

— Is there something in the present owner's social, religious or political connections that has helped his business succeed? And once he has left the business, is it probable that you will lose the customers that these connections have attracted?

— Will you have to assume the current lease, and does it seem to be satisfactory? Can it be renewed upon expiration? Does it include any unacceptable conditions?

— Are the key employees willing to stay and work for you?

Don't be afraid to ask the present owner these questions, or any others that may come to mind. Once James H. began asking them, it helped him organize his own thinking—and helped him avoid business ventures that could have been disastrous for him.

WHY IS THE BUSINESS FOR SALE?

James H. realized that probably the most important question listed above involved the reason(s) why the business was being sold. He considered it so critical that he not only asked the seller, but he asked anyone else who might have an idea—bankers, suppliers, neighbors, customers and employees.

Owners often told James that they were selling the business because of retirement or ailing health. But his own investigation sometimes revealed other reasons—the store was poorly located, the product being sold was of inferior quality, etc. If the product is bad, or the competition is too stiff, avoid the business. If the enterprise is being sold because it's been poorly managed, you should be able to reverse that, unless the seller's incompetence has irreparably damaged the business' reputation. And, of course, if you find out from the other businessmen on the block that a freeway is soon going to be built through the store you're interested in, obviously save your money for another business investment.

After seven months, James finally found a business that he decided to buy—a gun shop. "I have hunted all my life, and I know a lot about guns and rifles," says James. "I found this great little shop less than two miles from where I live.

"The man who sold the business to me had to move to a drier climate because of his health. His employees, who are all very knowledgeable, agreed to keep working for me. I don't think I lost a single customer because of the change in ownership. And a newspaper ad that I ran brought in some new customers."

Probably the biggest windfall of James' new business is his ammunition sales. Although ammunition is only a "sideline" in his store, its sales almost equal that of new and reconditioned guns and rifles. They are helping to make James' business a very lucrative one.

HOW MUCH SHOULD YOU PAY?

Probably the most difficult aspect of buying an existing business is determining how much it's worth. Overpaying for a business is not uncommon, since the buyer is so often incapable of calculating exactly what a business should cost. After all, if an enterprise is as fabulous as the seller claims, then maybe it's worth the asking price!

Your best defense against paying more than you should is to evaluate every record and receipt you can possibly obtain. And the best person to do this for you is an accountant or an auditor. Even though you'll be charged for this service, it will probably more than pay for itself if it makes it possible for you to bargain for a reduction in the purchase price of the business.

Have the accountant study the business' records for at least the previous three to four years. He should examine the business' gross margin or gross profit, and search for any hidden obligations (valid claims and contracts like liens, mortgages and back taxes). If you purchase the business and thus have to assume these liabilities, the sales price should take this factor into consideration. The accountant should also be able to provide you with an estimate of the worth of the assets being sold.

Use your accountant's figures as a negotiating tool when settling upon the final sales price. If the seller refuses to budge from his original price, which you may consider to be much too high, then you should probably look for another business.

Once you do find the right business, and agree to a mutually acceptable sales price, then hire an attorney to represent your interests when the final agreement is drawn up. It's advisable to take possession as soon as possible after the contract is signed.

BUYING A LIQUOR STORE

Lydia F. probably should have been a businesswoman all her life. She has always been independent, outgoing, aggressive, and bright. When she was in her mid-30s, and her children were old enough so as not to need constant attention, she and her sister almost opened up a small bakery. They laid out their plans well, but when it came to actually putting their ideas into motion, they never quite got them off the ground.

But 20 years later, Lydia and her husband, David, decided it was finally time for some self-fulfillment. He had been a liquor distributor for many years, and so he knew something about that type of business. Thus, the couple began thinking seriously about operating their own retail liquor store.

Lydia and David decided that they would buy an existing business if they could find a good one for sale. They reasoned that a going liquor store would already have a proven location, an inventory that was market-tested, and an established clientele. Also, the store would be generating income the day they took it over, thus immediately meeting expenses like rent, utilities, and so forth.

In his job, David constantly heard about liquor stores that were up for sale, and he and Lydia would check them out immediately. Finally they found one they liked—a perfect location, an attractive storefront appearance, a steady stream of customers, and admirable financial records.

"When we really started getting serious about this particular store, we hired a CPA to analyze the books," says Lydia. "And the figures were quite impressive. He took a close look at the sales growth, the operating expenses, and trends in accounts receivable. He finally recommended what he felt the selling price should be, and we took that to the owner."

Here's what the accountant calculated. As a rule, he felt that the sale price of a typical liquor store should be about two to three times its monthly gross sales, plus the inventory at cost. The monthly gross of the store in question was $10,550, so the following figures were put on paper:

2x monthly gross	$21,100
License market value	10,000
Total	$31,100
Inventory at cost	11,027
Selling price	$42,127

"At first, it seemed like a lot of money to me," recalls Lydia. "We figured we'd have to borrow most of it, and I just hated the thought of being that much in debt.

"But our accountant helped us calculate what our repayment schedule would be on a bank loan, and it was clear that we would have no trouble making the payments, and still be able to take home a comfortable sum of money to live on each week.

"We bought the liquor store for exactly $22 more than what our accountant had recommended. And things have worked out well. We have no complaints. Business is great!"

KEEPING THE CUSTOMERS SATISFIED

One of the biggest concerns of small businessmen taking over an existing enterprise is how to hold onto the store's regular customers. A store may have had excellent monthly sales figures when you bought it, but if you lose many of the customers who used to shop there, the price you paid for the store may not be quite the bargain you had thought it was.

Probably the best way to keep the regular customers coming back is to make some personal contact with them. Let them know who you are, and any improvements you've made in the business that they may find appealing.

Let's assume, for instance, that the previous owner has left you a list of names, addresses and phone numbers of his regular customers. Why not send each of them a leaflet through the mail, announcing a "change-of-ownership sale" for "our regular customers"? Make them feel special, as if they are as much of a VIP now as when the store was owned by someone else.

Learn as quickly as possible the tastes and buying habits of these regular customers, and gear your sales around their preferences. Drop them a handwritten note a few days before a sale, letting them know that you've arranged it with them in mind.

Another technique is to send "reminders" to regular customers. Let's say, for example, that you have bought an existing juvenile shoe store. Why not send a postcard to mothers, suggesting that it's time to bring in their child for "a free size checkup"? Of if you're the new owner of an auto repair shop, post cards can let regular customers know that it's time for a normal 3000-mile lubrication.

Michael N. bought a going auto maintenance center, and sent the following card to the customers who had regularly frequented the establishment before it was his:

**I've just assumed ownership of Superior Auto Re-
pairs. I'd like you to know that your patronage will be as
valued now as in the past. Please drop by sometime to say
hello, and, with this card, we will put your automobile
through a complete diagnostic test for only $8—half the
regular price.**

**Incidentally, as a new service to our customers, we
are now open evenings on Mondays. And a free pick-up
and delivery service is available.**

Sincerely,

Another effective technique used by some new businessmen is to
actually telephone regular customers, and informally introduce themselves. Particularly during bad weather or slow seasons, when you may
have some spare moments, why not make good use of the time this
way.

Here are some of the things that can be included in your conversation with these customers, to let them know you're interested in
them and their opinions:

— Tell them your name, and how long you've been running the
business.
— Invite them to come in for a free cup of coffee, and to look at
any new merchandise you may be featuring.
— Tell them about any upcoming sales that they may find of
interest.
— Ask them if they'd like to see any changes in the store's
policies, including the services it provides or the products it
sells.

The Secret of Art A.'s Success

Many customers frequent stores that don't have the lowest prices
in town, simply because of the personal service that is offered. If you
can show your clientele that you really care about them, and have
considerable knowledge about the products you're selling, they'll
probably remain as loyal customers.

Art A., who recently bought an existing paint store, takes the time to learn the names of each of his regular customers. "When they come in, I introduce myself and ask them their names," he says. "I'm lucky in that I usually remember their names the next time I see them. And it impresses them that I care enough about my customers to be able to say 'Hello, Mr. Jones' or 'Good morning, Mrs. Smith,' rather than having to say, 'Hello, sir.'"

CHANGING THE BUSINESS' NAME

Generally, there's no reason to change the name of the business that you are taking over. For instance, if you're buying an enterprise called Sunset Nursery, and it happens to be located on a street called Sunset Avenue, it would be appropriate to leave the name just as it is. After all, most of its regular customers know it by the name, so why confuse them? A change in name may cause them to think that there's also been a change in products or service.

Even if the business carries a personal name like Frank's Garden Center, it still might be wise to leave it as is—even if Frank will no longer be around. Once again, customers know the business by that name, and a change may persuade them that there are other changes in the store as well.

The one exception to this advice is if you're purchasing a business that had a negative reputation when you acquired it. If the store had more unhappy customers under the previous owner than happy ones, then you should change the name and try for a new start.

STREAMLINING THE ACQUIRED BUSINESS

When Jeremy T. became the new owner of Coast Stationery Supplies, he almost had to laugh the first week that the business was his. Among hundreds of other items, the store sold a complete array of bookkeeping forms and supplies. Yet the previous owners had never made use of these very items—the forms that they were selling themselves—and thus their records were more confusing than complete.

So Jeremy decided that his first real "behind-the-scenes" chore would be to organize the records into a presentable and understandable system.

"First of all," says Jeremy, "I verified the inventory that was made when I bought the business. Then I went through the pile of receipts to determine what items were selling well, and which ones weren't selling at all.

"Frankly, some of the best-selling items were repeatedly out of stock. The previous owner never anticipated what he would be selling, and so he never ordered a product until he was completely out of it. Not only does that policy cause unhappy customers, but it chases them to other stationery stores for good."

Jeremy T.'s system of organization was certainly not complex. In fact, he essentially just followed the simple directions which were enclosed with the bookkeeping and inventory forms that his store sold. Once he had matters in order, he phased out certain items that weren't selling, and emphasized the more popular ones. Within a year, Jeremy had increased the sales volume of his store by 35 percent. And he expects those figures to be even better as more people hear about the "new look" of his store.

CHAPTER 7

A Money-Making Home Business

"Independence!"

The word can be used many ways, but when spoken by a small businessman, it carries with it a presumption of freedom and self-reliance that is exhilerating. For every American who is running his own small business, there are probably five or ten who wish they were, but who simply lack the courage to move out on their own.

Because you've already read this far in this book, you obviously are more than a dreamer. You may have absorbed dozens of ideas that you'll put into action in the upcoming months. And with determination and perseverence, that action can bring you an annual income higher than you've ever earned before.

Although many successful small businessmen must drive to the office each morning, there are others who only have to take a few steps from their bedroom or kitchen to go to work. They have the ideal situation—their own business operating out of their home.

6 ADVANTAGES TO A HOME BUSINESS

Working at home is enticing for many reasons. You can probably think of some of the advantages yourself, including the following:

(1) The home office is incredibly convenient. You have no rush-hour traffic on the streets and highways to contend with, nor must you awaken early enough each morning to allow for commuting time to work.

(2) Working at home allows you to be wonderfully flexible in planning your day. For instance, if you project working an eight-hour day, you can arrange those eight hours so as to permit time for other activities. If you want to spend the morning at your son's school, watching him perform in the college play, you certainly have that option. After all, you have no worries about an office building turning

off its lights at 6 p.m. Or if you must schedule a dentist appointment for mid-afternoon, you can do so with the knowledge that you have no one to answer to but yourself, and thus can set your own working hours. Or you can plan to have lunch with your family every day, and not have to think about punching a timeclock.

(3) You don't have the trouble and expense of finding and renting office space. Not only have offices become extremely expensive these days, but it's also difficult finding one with the specifications that you need. Look at that back bedroom or empty garage space at home—maybe one or both can be converted into the office you'll need.

(4) For individuals who are shut-ins, a home business is a means to live a full, productive and independent life without feeling restricted by their immobility. Being confined to one's home is no real detriment when the office is right on the premises.

(5) The businessman who works at home is usually thought of quite highly by his neighbors. You are envied and considered important for being able to accomplish something which relatively few people do—working right out of your own house.

(6) There are many tax breaks that you'll be entitled to as an at-home businessman. These tax advantages will be discussed later in this chapter, but for now, keep in mind that your home office will look more attractive than ever on April 15 every year.

BREEDING CANARIES AT HOME

Mary R. recalls her childhood as if it were only yesterday—even though it was actually many years ago. She was fortunate enough to grow up in a family filled with love, but unlucky enough to be born in an era before the polio vaccine was perfected.

As a teenager, Mary was afflicted with polio. Although she is not confined to a bed or a wheelchair today, she has never walked normally since the ailment struck. Mary R. certainly doesn't consider herself an invalid, but neither can she move about with the ease of most people.

Thus, when a friend suggested that Mary breed canaries for a living, it sounded like a superb idea. The business could be operated completely out of her home, and the sight and sound of birds seemed particularly attractive.

Mary set aside a back room in her home for the canaries. Ten years ago, in the spring, she bought some cages and obtained her first group of birds from another breeder. She had been told to expect between six and ten baby birds from each breeding pair. And that was precisely the way things turned out.

A subscription to a periodical called *Cage Bird Magazine* (3449 N. Western Ave., Chicago, Ill. 60618) provided Mary with many important breeding tips—from how to administer vitamin supplements to the birds, to how to check the eggs for fertilization. She also read a variety of books on the subject, including *Canary Breeding for Beginners* by Kyle Onstott. After the first year, and with several nests active, she felt like a real pro. And her biggest expense now is bird feed—about $30 per year for each breeding pair.

Mary sells her birds at wholesale to pet stores—not only in her community, but in other parts of the nation. She has learned how easy it is to ship the birds in specially designed mailing cages. She sells the male canaries for $20 to $25 each, and females for about half that. She sells literally hundreds of them each year.

Incidentally, Mary's business has introduced her to other people who breed canaries, as well as many who simply love birds. Along with her newfound friends, she has started a bird club in her city, and meetings are held monthly right in her own living room. For Mary R., working at home has left her—and her birds—singing with joy.

THE RIGHT BUSINESS AT THE RIGHT TIME

One reason why Mary R. is succeeding at her home business is that she chose one that meets a current need. People who live in cities—particularly apartment dwellers who don't have the space for dogs and cats—are turning to birds for pets. The high price of canaries is directly a result of the heavy demand and relatively low supply of them.

For a home business—or any other type of business, for that matter—your chances for success will depend significantly upon whether you've chosen the right business at the right time. Be aware of the type of products and services that are needed in your community. Scan the classified ads of local newspapers, and listen to what neighbors have to say. Do any of their needs or desires tie in with a home business that you could start?

How Charles H. Found His Opportunity

Charles H. was waiting in a grocery store checkout line when he overheard a conversation between two women standing next to him. They were complaining about the "outrageous" costs of auto repairs. One had just spent over $300 having some repairs done on her car. The other was angry over a $51 bill for a tuneup.

As he drove home, Charles began to think how he might be able to cash in on the public discontent with high auto repair costs. Charles had grown up with cars, and knew as much about them as anything else. He had always done most of the repair work on his own car. So, he thought, why not pass some of that knowledge on to other people, by teaching auto repair classes at his own home?

Charles and his wife told a few of their neighbors about his plans, and the reaction was enthusiastic. Three weeks later, when Charles began his instruction, 14 people—both men and women— were in attendance. The class sessions were held Monday, Wednesday and Friday evenings for two consecutive weeks—at five dollars per person per session. That first group of 14 ended up paying "tuition" totaling $420.

As word of Charles' classes spread, his phone began ringing with regularity. Before long, he was teaching his classes six days a week— Monday, Wednesday and Friday evenings, and Tuesday, Thursday and Saturday mornings.

Eventually, Charles began running a small classified ad in the community newspaper, which attracted more "students." "I'm making money, and in the process, I'm teaching people how to save money. It's a great situation."

FIND A BUSINESS YOU LIKE

It's foolish to enter into a business that you don't enjoy. And that is particularly true of a home business. When you work at home, you're always around the business, even during your leisure hours. There's no such thing as completely leaving the office for the day and totally escaping the business. It's always just a few feet away in another room.

Imagine, for example, how Mary R. could maintain her sanity if she hated the sight and sound of canaries? Also, would Charles be as happy as he is if he hated cars and the dirty hands that accompany repairing them?

Thus, finding a business that's right for the times is only one factor in a successful home enterprise. You must also find one that you enjoy. If you choose one that you'll lose interest in very quickly, that eventual lack of enthusiasm will probably be reflected in the business itself. There will likely be a decrease in quality of your product or service, followed by a drop in the number of customers you attract.

5 STEPS TO CHOOSING A SUCCESSFUL HOME BUSINESS

To sum up, then, here are five tips on selecting a business that is destined for success:

(1) Choose one that fulfills a definite community need. Ask your friends and neighbors what products and services they feel need to be met, and think in those directions.

(2) Check the Yellow Pages to see if other businesses exist similar to the one you are considering. If there are already many of them in your vicinity, choose another type of enterprise.

(3) Select a business that you will enjoy not only now, but also several years down the road. If you're not enthusiastic about your endeavor, your chances of success are dim.

(4) Read the trade magazines relating to the home business you're planning to enter. For instance, if you're thinking of opening up a shoe repair business at home, read a few issues of a journal like *Master Shoe Rebuilder Magazine* (15 Stonybrook Dr., Levittown, Pa. 19055). Or if you're interested in launching your own camera repair business at home, pick up a copy or two of *The Camera Craftsman* (2000 W. Union Ave., Englewood, Co. 80110). These trade magazines run articles on trends in their particular fields. If they project a promising future for the type of business you have in mind, your prospects for success are very bright.

(5) Once you've made up your mind, jump into your new business wholeheartedly. Make the decisions with confidence that you feel have to be made. Nothing is worse than a baseball player not swinging at strike three because he is afraid of missing the ball. Likewise, don't be the type of home businessman who is afraid to take action because he's fearful that it might be the wrong type of action. Everyone makes mistakes, and we learn from all of them. But if you don't act, you won't accomplish anything, except to reinforce your own indecisiveness.

ORGANIZING YOUR HOUSEHOLD FOR SUCCESS

One of the most difficult facets of running a business at home is rearranging your house to accommodate your enterprise. Obviously, you need space to work. Depending on the type of business, it could just be a desk in the corner of the bedroom, or an entire room or more.

Whatever you decide is necessary, keep in mind that your home office usually needs to be a place free of distractions and interruptions. Imagine trying to operate a typing business when you are constantly being disturbed by children playing outside or dogs barking incessantly. So choose a room, or a corner of a room, that has some semblence of solitude and quietness.

Basement offices are often ideal. They are separated from the commotion of the rest of the house, and removed from screaming neighborhood children, noisy washing machines, and blaring television sets.

A good idea, once you have chosen the location of your home office, is to put a lock on the door of the room that you're using. This is not intended primarily as a deterrent against burglars, although it will certainly serve that purpose. More importantly, the lock will keep children and/or grandchildren out of a room where they shouldn't be. Youngsters can make havoc out of an organized file cabinet if left free to play with it for a few minutes. Save yourself the heartache of having your papers and records left in disarray by investing in a simple lock to keep unwanted people away.

Incidentally, when you're working at home, you may find that your wife (or husband) sees nothing wrong with visiting your desk for a few minutes every hour or so. Nothing can be more distracting. Just because you're working at home, that doesn't mean that you shouldn't work in a businesslike atmosphere. Keep the door to your office closed when you're working, and create some family ground rules that you're not to be disturbed short of an emergency. You'll never get anything accomplished otherwise.

STARTING WITH MINIMUM CAPITAL

Because there's no need to rent office space when you're working at home, a business operating out of the house can cost considerably less money to start. But your economizing doesn't necessarily stop there. The nature of home businesses is such that they are frequently less expensive to start in many other ways. When you start a home typing service, your only necessary investment is a good electric typewriter. If you want to launch a tax preparation business, all you need is an inexpensive electronic calculator and a pencil or pen.

Thus, a home business is perfect for someone who has only a little money to spend to get the enterprise underway. And you can make up for your lack of capital with hard work and dedication to the business. By putting in time instead of dollars, you can often do just as well as a businessman who is investing hundreds or even thousands of dollars more than you. Eventually, when your business is doing well and you're making money, you can buy the business "luxuries" that will allow you to take things a bit more leisurely. You'll be able to afford the best tools, the best electronic equipment, or the best chemicals. But for now, do as much of the work as possible yourself, using manpower instead of money-power to get your business moving initially.

How Dinah M. Overcame a Barrier

By all means, don't feel insecure because you're starting small, and because you're working with less capital than a competitor in the community. Persistence and patience can compensate for your limited finances. Take the case of Dinah M., who longed to start a business, but simply didn't think she could afford to do so. She had always believed in herself, but she had let her financial situation hold her back all her life.

But Dinah, with the encouragement of friends, is now operating a successful home business, that required almost no capital at all to start. She is making money at a craft that she has actually been doing for years—candlemaking. She already had the basic equipment she needed to get started—waxes, molds, wicks, dyes—and the cost of purchasing more is minimal. Her candles, which she wholesales to local gift shops, retail for as much as $10 to $25 each.

"I'm becoming quite creative with the type of candles I'm making now, and I'm amazed at the demand for them," says Dinah. "One of the gift shop owners who I do business with has told me that she can probably sell as much merchandise as I can supply her with. That's a great feeling—not only from a financial point of view, but as far as self-fulfillment goes, too."

Dinah gets ideas for her most usual candles from a trade journal in the field, *The Journal of the American Candlemaker* (P.O. Box 1203, Santa Cruz, Cal. 95060). In the journal, she has learned of supply houses through which she can buy various candlemaking equipment. She has seen her business grow, and feels her only limitation now is the amount of time she wants to spend with it.

SETTING YOUR GOALS

Once your home business is underway, you should take out a piece of paper and set some realistic goals for yourself. How much money did you make in the first few weeks that the business was operating? Can you honestly expect things to get better, and if so, how much better? Will the need or desire for your product or service increase in the years ahead, or stay about the same? What steps can you take (advertising, distributing leaflets) to let even more people know that your home business exists?

In the early stages of your business, probably the most important action you can take to ensure prosperity is to provide the best possible product or service you can. If your initial customers are satisfied, word-of-mouth will bring you new customers in a short time. The best advertising—a happy customer—costs you nothing at all. So even if the first few weeks do not come up to your expectations from a financial standpoint, stick with it. If you're offering a sound and well-made item, and one that is needed, momentum will eventually start building. And once the money begins accumulating in large amounts, you'll be happy that any apprehension you felt at the beginning didn't get the best of you.

GETTING THE FIRST CUSTOMERS

Ronald G. recalls very well the early days of his locksmith business. His office was in his garage, and working there was ideal—except that he didn't have many customers in the first few weeks. "I wasn't the only locksmith in town, and getting the word out that I was available wasn't the easiest thing in the world," he recalls.

Finally, Ronald decided to go directly to his customers. In his free time during the day, he took out the Yellow Pages and made phone calls to businesses in the community which he felt were potential clients. "I was a little hesitant at first, but my reception by almost everyone was very cordial," he says. "I introduced myself, told them the services I was offering, and played up the point that my fees were lower than anyone else in town. I also suggested that I come by and look over their own security situation, and see if they needed any new or better locks. I quickly began accumulating customers, who later called me on a regular basis whenever they needed my services."

At the same time, Ronald ran a small display ad in the local weekly newspaper, which said:

RONALD'S LOCK & SAFE SERVICE
All types of lock, safe & key
work done expertly and quickly.
Lowest rates in town.
As near as your phone.
Call now for residential and
business service.
759-3841

The ad ran in the newspaper for four consecutive weeks. The response was incredible. In the crime-rampant society we live in, it seems as though everyone is worried about keeping intruders away from his home or office. So once people knew that Ronald's business existed, his customer list increased dramatically. And the total price of the four ads—$140.

"One of the first callers who responded to my ad needed eight new locks in his house," says Ronald. "That paid for the ads right there. The rest was gravy!"

TAKE A DAY OFF EVERY WEEK

Talk to anyone with a home business that he thoroughly enjoys, and he'll probably tell you that one of the most difficult facets of working at home is knowing when to stop. When do you leave the desk and move into the living room to spend the rest of the day with the family?

Many work-at-homers spend more time on the job than do their counterparts who work in offices. Those who work in offices leave their businesses behind when they go home each night. But the home businessman never gets that far away. And if he's excited about his work, the temptation is great to keep on working late into the night, instead of watching TV with the family or helping the teenagers with their homework.

Well, don't let that happen to you. If your business prospers, but at the expense of your family life, it's not worth it. Put yourself on a schedule that you can live with. Let's say, for instance, that you decide that you're going to quit working at 6:30 p.m. every day. Although exceptions will arise now and then—like on the day when you have a particularly big order, or on the morning when you take the grandchildren to the zoo instead of working—generally abide by that rule. You'll find that once it becomes routine, both you and your family will add a feeling of normalcy to your lives.

Also, decide to take at least one day off each week—preferably Saturday or Sunday, when the entire family can be together. Even if your youngsters are already grown, Sunday is a great day to visit them and the grandchildren. And if you're single, you should still set aside a day for yourself, when you can relax alone or with friends, and just unwind from the week's activities.

4 WAYS TO SAVE ON TAXES

As someone who uses his home as the primary place of business, you can take advantage of many significant tax breaks that will ease Uncle Sam's bite on your income every April. Take note of the following four tax tips, that apply to you as a work-at-home businessman.

1. If you rent your home, you can deduct a percentage of your rent and utilities as a legitimate business expense. Let's say, for instance, that you have your office in one room of your six-room house. Well, you can deduct one-sixth of your monthly rent and one-sixth of your electricity bill. So if you pay $240-a-month for rent, you can deduct $40 per month—or $480 per year—as a business expense. Likewise, $4 of your $24 per month electricity bill is tax-deductible. If you own your home, you can also avail yourself of tax savings by taking a depreciation deduction equal to a percentage of what you originally paid for the house. You can also deduct a percentage of your utilities.

2. When you have business-related improvements done to your house—whether you own it or rent it—these are tax-deductible. For instance, if you paint or repair the room that you use exclusively for your office, these costs are fully deductible. Even if you repair the roof, or paint the house's exterior, you can still deduct a pro rata portion of these expenses.

3. You probably have homeowner's insurance, or renter's insurance, on your residence. Here again, a percentage of your annual premium is tax-deductible.

4. You are also entitled to the same tax savings that all other self-employed individuals are, including those that are applicable to people who work away from home. For instance, you can claim a percentage of your automobile operating costs as a deduction. This is normally claimed at a standard mileage rate of 15 cents per mile for the first 15,000 miles of business use each year, and 10 cents a mile for each succeeding mile of business use each year. Also, if you pay salaries to your wife, children or other dependents who work for you

in your business, you can deduct these wages, often without changing their status as full exemptions. In addition, don't forget to claim a depreciation deduction for the equipment you use in your day-to-day business, including desks, file cabinets and tools.

A SECOND BUSINESS AT HOME

Many people think of home businesses as a part-time enterprise. However, in more cases than not, they require full-time attention in order to achieve real money-making status.

Still, there are many instances of individuals running home businesses as a secondary venture. They are either already employed full-time by someone else, or they already have a small business of their own *away* from home. In an effort to hike their income as high as possible, they start a new business at home, hoping to turn it into the source of a sizable second income.

How Shirley P. Launched a Second Business

Shirley P., for instance, owns a small dress shop in her community, which has built up an established clientele over the years. The business seemed secure, and she contemplated starting a new type of enterprise. She finally decided to take advantage of her artistic talents, which had been dormant for 20 years. She went into her attic and found an array of materials that she had designed in the past—brochures, catalogs, letterheads, emblems, charts and ads. She made herself a portfolio, and began calling on advertising agencies in the city, looking for free-lance work. She was lucky. Her artistic efforts ended up earning her $5100 the first year—on a very part-time basis working out of her house in the evenings.

If you're thinking of launching a second business and basing it at home, be sure that your first business is firmly established. Don't jeopardize your original enterprise by channeling your energies into a second one. But if the first one is stable and capable of thriving without your constant attention, it's foolish not to think about a second one. It's a way to eventually add considerable amounts of money to your income.

CHAPTER 8

Profitable Home Businesses
After Age 50

As you've seen in the previous chapter, the types of money-making businesses that you can operate in your home are as endless as your imagination. You can probably think of several that are particularly appropriate for you, based upon your own talents and interests, plus the particular needs of your community.

However, if you are uncertain about what type of enterprise to pursue, first make a list of all the things you do well. Then alongside each of them, write a home business or two that corresponds to that skill. For example, if you can speak and write French, you're quite capable of tutoring it in your home—not only to students from the local high school or college, but to neighbors who are planning a business or pleasure trip to France or Canada.

If you have talent in the kitchen, you might think about opening up your own home bakery, preparing cakes for weddings, or pies for local bazaars.

No matter what home business you ultimately select, you will enjoy the extraordinary benefits of working where you live. As you recall from the last chapter, you'll have neither the worry nor the expense of renting an office, because all the space you'll require is right in your own home. There will never be a need to battle crowded streets and highways on your way to and from work. And the time you might have spent commuting to work can be devoted to your home business. Even 30 extra minutes a day (on a five-day-a-week schedule) can add up to more than 100 extra hours of work per year—hours which can be turned into dollars.

This chapter will describe typical businesses you can run from your home—all of which can bring you annual incomes of $12,000 or more. If you're sincerely interested in money-making opportunities, read about each of these businesses, while keeping your own skills in mind. You may find one or more that is right for you, and which can guarantee you a comfortable income and a secure future.

EARNING BIG MONEY AS A TELEVISION REPAIRMAN

Marshall W. had been an automobile mechanic for 24 years when he decided to go into business for himself. But believing that the required investment would be prohibitive if he launched his own car repair shop, he decided instead to work out of his home as a television repairman.

Six months before leaving his auto mechanic's job, he began taking night courses in TV repairing at California Trade Technical School near his home. When he graduated from the school, he rearranged the garage in his house to give him some room to work at his newly found trade.

Within a day after quitting his mechanic's job and starting his TV repair business, he had his first customer—a neighbor who had a second-hand TV that had been on the blink for months. An advertisement in the community newspaper brought him other customers, and before long, he was averaging $425 a week net income. Marshall was working hard, but he was also earning more money than he ever had before.

Obtaining Spare Parts

If you live in a city where there is already a TV parts wholesaler, you can launch your own TV repair service and keep your overhead to a minimum, since you won't have to stock up on parts, but can just buy them when you need them. Marshall lives just an eight-minute drive from the nearest wholesale TV parts store, so he did not at all feel the need to buy a complete inventory of parts. He had to purchase some basic tools and testing equipment, but they cost under $350.

TV repairing can be a very lucrative home business. Many repairmen make much more than Marshall W., with incomes ranging into the $500 to $600-per-week category.

There are hundreds of schools that teach TV repairing, and most have evening classes. But even if none exists in your area, you can take a convenient correspondence course and learn everything you need to know via the mails.

Once your business is open, run an ad in your community newspaper that tells readers simply and precisely the service you offer.

Also, have some leaflets printed up that you can insert in the mailboxes of your neighbors. Be sure to list any special services you offer. For example, can you promise same-day service? Will you offer a guarantee? Do you charge less than nearby competitors?

Remember that quality work and courtesy can make your business blossom. TV is here to stay, and so are competent TV repairmen.

FINDING SUCCESS IN TAX RETURN PREPARATION

If you have always had a particular aptitude for working with numbers, then you may find a tax return preparation business a profitable one. It will take a bit of study before you'll feel knowledgeable enough to handle income tax forms for others, but once you've mastered the contemporary tax laws, you could make over $20,000 for just four months of work a year.

To begin with, contact your local Internal Revenue Office and ask for a free copy of *Your Federal Income Tax*, a 192-page booklet that explains in plain language the art of preparing an income tax return. After you've read and digested this material, then ask the IRS for copies of its specialty publications, which discuss various tax problems in more depth: e.g., *Tax Information for Visitors to the United States, Tax Benefits for Older Americans, Tax Information on Selling Your Home*, etc.

Opening a Tax Return Service

Once you feel you've mastered the material—or at least know where it is so you can refer to it whenever necessary—then make plans to open up your own tax office at home. In January of a new tax year, let your friends and neighbors know of your availability to handle their taxes. You can also run an ad in your local newspapers, and distribute flyers throughout your community.

Most tax returns are actually fairly simple to complete. The IRS will provide you with all the forms you need, and once you've done a few of them, they will become simpler. If you run into any problems along the way, IRS personnel will answer any questions you have over the phone. You can call them toll-free at 800-242-4500.

You can charge as little as $10 for the simplest of income tax returns. As they become more complex, raise your fee to $20, $30, $40, $50 and up.

In order to avoid the April 15 rush, encourage your customers to contact you as early as possible in the tax season. If you can spread out your accounts over a four-month period, you will be able to work in a much more relaxed atmosphere. But nevertheless, be prepared to put in extra hours during the first two weeks of April.

A LUCRATIVE HOME PHOTOGRAPHY STUDIO

Vance A. has always enjoyed photography, and he became so proficient at his hobby that he won several local picture-taking contests. The rear bathroom in his house was where he developed all his own photos, and the creative process of shooting, developing and printing was one of the most satisfying things in his life.

So it was only natural for Vance to someday become a professional photographer. Using his house as his studio, it was relatively simple to launch his own portrait photography business.

Vance's first customers were the parents of neighborhood children, who paid him $30 for a series of four color portraits of their youngsters. Each parent and child would come to Vance's house, where he would shoot a roll of film. By the next day, he would have a proof sheet ready for the parent to examine. Once the final selections were made, he printed the portraits within another day's time.

Before long, word of Vance's talents had traveled throughout the community. A neighbor kindly announced his service at a local PTA meeting, which brought him a flurry of new customers. A small ad in the Yellow Pages helped, too. In his first year, his net income was $12,200.

What You Will Need to Start

When you start your own home photography studio, you don't necessarily need a fully equipped darkroom. In fact, until your business gets off the ground, there's no necessity of taking the risk of investing $700 or more in darkroom equipment. Instead, your developing and processing work can be sent out daily to a professional processing facility in your city.

Attract customers any way you can. An inexpensive flyer announcing your talents can be distributed in shopping centers. If you're interested in photographing weddings, be on the lookout for newspaper announcements of engagements, and contact the bride's family, offering your services. For 30 color photos of a wedding, including an album, you can charge from $200 to $250.

You can also keep abreast of confirmations, christenings, Bar Mitzvahs, etc. by checking church calendars in your community. These are all good outlets for your photo talents.

ESTABLISHING A TELEPHONE ANSWERING SERVICE

There are probably many businessmen and companies in your community needing their phones answered at times when no one is in their offices. Physicians, lawyers, TV repairmen, plumbers, electricians, insurance salesmen, and writers are all prime potential customers for a telephone answering service, operated out of your home. If there is not already one in your community, or if you are aware of some dissatisfaction with the existing services, then you have an opportunity to cash in with such a business of your own.

It is very possible for you to earn well over $20,000 a year with your own telephone answering service, but you will also have to put up more of an initial investment than some of the other home businesses described in this chapter. Still, the potential profits may be worth the early risks.

Buying Equipment

The biggest expense involves special electrical equipment which must be installed in your home, including line-terminating apparatus and a switchboard. The equipment itself can be rented, but the installation charge of the phone company can run into several hundred dollars. The phone company also requires a deposit of about $200 to cover the cost of any damage to the equipment. Other costs, including advertising, may delay your break-even point to three or four months after you open for business.

The best way to obtain customers is to send out printed leaflets, or a personal letter, to prospective clients. An advertisement in the Yellow Pages is also advisable:

VALLEY ANSWERING BUREAU
Never miss another call.
We're Fast
We're Friendly
We're Dependable
Call about our reasonable rates.
572-3301

Typical fees for answering services are $17 to $35 per month, for a specified number of messages a month (usually between 70 and 100). Each additional message carries a fee of 5 to 10 cents. Other special services, like wakeup calls, also cost extra.

To run an answering service properly, you should be able to take messages accurately. You must also be polite at all times, even to the rudest of callers. In addition, be willing to stay within hearing range of your switchboard during business hours, or you'll probably miss some calls and lose your credibility among clients.

Public relations is a very important factor in the success of a telephone answering service. You'll find that customers will keep your service indefinitely as long as you are doing a good job. Loyalty of clientele is quite common, so this can be a very secure business as long as you are polite and efficient.

Incidentally, once your business is underway, the best way to attract new customers is just to answer the phone properly. When individuals call one of your current clients, and find that you answer his phone quickly and take messages accurately, they may consequently become a customer of yours.

For further information about a phone answering business, you can obtain a free copy of *Telephone Answering Service* from your local Small Business Administration Office, or from the SBA's national headquarters (Washington, D.C. 20416).

SUCCEEDING IN PLANT CARE AT HOME

Robin S. and Martha J., two sisters who love plants, have made that love the foundation for their "Planet Earth" plant business, which they operate out of their homes. They not only sell a wide variety of plants, but they also offer emergency care for ailing plants, "baby-sit" for plants whose owners are on vacation, and teach about plant care in classes in their living rooms.

Their reward for their home-grown business is a lot of happy plants, plus an annual income of $27,000, that the sisters divide equally between them.

In this era when plants are so popular, a home business revolving around growing greenery is an enterprise with immense profit potential. Nature does most of the work in growing the plants, so all you have to do is find customers who will give them good homes.

If you have a big backyard, you can grow the plants that you'll eventually sell. If not, there is probably a wholesale nursery in your city where you can buy plants very inexpensively. Plants that retail for $15 can be bought at these wholesale outlets for $3 to $4. Because your overhead is so low when working out of your home, you can sell that same plant for $8 and still make a nice profit, while your competitor may have to stick to his $15 price to offset his higher business expenses.

Begin selling your plants to friends and neighbors, and depend on word-of-mouth to propel your business forward. Drop a brief letter to several local physicians and businessmen, letting them know that you are available to decorate their office with plants. Once you have been hired to decorate a few offices, then it will be easier to get other customers.

You might consider offering all your customers a photocopied sheet, explaining the best way to care for plants. Although plants are sold at many places, few businesses offer any advice on how to keep the greenery alive and flourishing. This extra added service may bring you many return customers.

UTILIZING YOUR ARTISTIC TALENTS

Your artistic talents can make you a lucrative living at home, particularly in this era when items like leather goods and macrame are so popular. If you have some type of talent—from rug weaving to artificial flower arranging to making costume jewelry—you should consider using it to earn a living.

You can make these items for private customers as well as for stores. In cities like San Francisco, local artists are welcome to sell their wares at local parks on weekends. Swap meets are another likely place to sell your goods. Your income is limited only by your time and creativity, and some hard-working craftsmen are earning $20,000 a year from their creations.

When placing a pricetag on your products, charge for the price of your materials plus $3 to $5 per hour for labor. Leather sandals can sell for as high as $50 a pair. Leather boots can bring four or five times as much. Leather belts sell for $20 apiece.

Individuals who make a lot of money in this field sometimes launch a mail-order branch of their business. Place ads in regional magazines, and orders may come pouring in if your products and prices are attractive.

Making $14,400 as a Home Tutor

Roberta C. made $14,400 in 1974, and all because 30 years ago, she learned to teach problem children to read. Roberta had attended the University of Southern California in the mid-1940s, and although she dropped out before graduation to get married, she had taken several education classes, and acquired the skills needed to teach reading.

Once her children were grown, Roberta sought a second income for her family, and she was naturally drawn to the teaching of reading—all in her own home. She charges $5 per half-hour, and $8 per hour (the going rates in her town). And in this era when there are so many "Johnnys who can't read," she has no trouble attracting customers.

Roberta found her first clients by contacting local elementary schools, and letting both principals and teachers know of her availability. She also put notices on the bulletin boards of local supermarkets. Before long, she had a busy schedule of students, and word-of-mouth brought her even more.

If you have expertise in a particular area, take advantage of that knowledge and channel it into a lucrative private tutoring business in your home. For example, if you are proficient in music, why not teach music lessons to youngsters in your community? In every city, there are parents eager to introduce their children to the world of music via lessons on the piano, guitar, violin, clarinet, bass or a dozen other popular instruments. You can charge anywhere from $5 to $15 for a one-hour lesson.

Except in the case of piano lessons, your students will bring their own instruments with them, so there's no need for you to invest in this potentially expensive hardware. Incidentally, if you make arrangements in advance, some music stores will pay you a commission on any instruments they sell to students you have sent to them. So find a music store in your neighborhood with a wide selection of instruments at reasonable prices, and ask them if they'll be willing to pay you, say, 10 per cent commission for sales to your students.

In teaching music, try to avoid disturbing your neighbors as much as possible. If you live in an apartment building, ask the other tenants if they'd be willing to tolerate the music from your apartment for a few hours each day.

Expertise in a foreign language is also a highly marketable skill. There may be hundreds of businessmen in your city who, in preparation for an overseas trip, need a quick conversation course in Spanish, French, German, Italian or Japanese. Your customers could also include individuals planning world vacations, and who want to be able to get along in a foreign land without referring to a phrasebook before every sentence.

High school and college students, too, may need special tutoring in the foreign language they are studying—particularly just before final exams. Private lessons can range from $5 to $10 an hour. You can also teach groups at a reduced per-person rate.

Find your customers in a variety of ways. An advertisement in the classified section of the local newspaper will probably attract some clients:

FRENCH TUTORING available for businessmen, travelers, students. $8 hour. Call 823-7421

Let the schools in your neighborhood know of your tutoring services. Put notices in PTA bulletins, or pin them up in teachers' lounges, as well as supermarkets and other places where people might notice them.

If you're offering music lessons, ask local music stores to tell their customers of your availability.

CLIPPING NEWSPAPERS FOR BIG PROFITS

There are 1820 daily newspapers in the United States, and more than 9000 weeklies. When you combine that with the fact that tens of thousands of businesses have an acute interest in particular articles that these newspapers run, you can see how a successful home business could be launched by supplying individuals and companies with the particular articles they want.

A clipping service bureau certainly is not the easiest of businesses to set in motion, but in time it can be one of the most lucrative, earning well over $20,000 annually.

The competition in your area will determine what chances you have at success. If there are now no clipping bureaus in your region, then you may have a good opportunity for prosperity. But before you decide for certain, phone various people in your town—like advertising agents, local celebrities, businessmen, politicians and public relations agents. Are they interested in having you send them newspaper articles about themselves or about any subject they choose?

If you get some positive response and can line up about 25 to 30 clients, then it's certainly worth launching your business. Subscribe to about 30 to 40 key newspapers—both local and out-of-town—and a cross section of daily and weekly papers.

When the newspapers begin arriving, read through them carefully but quickly, searching for articles about your clients or subjects in which they have expressed an interest. You can charge them a flat $25-a-month fee, plus 15¢ to 20¢ for every clipping you send them.

Once you get your business rolling, use every opportunity to expand it. For example, if a local weekly prints an article on a new Tom McAn shoe store, clip the story and send it to the national offices of Thom McAn. They probably haven't seen the article, particularly if it ran in a small town newspaper. Tell them you'd be happy to send them further articles, and quote them your prices. You'll probably attract many customers this way.

As your client list grows, you'll be able to afford to subscribe to more and more newspapers, and make your services even more thorough and thus more attractive to prospective clients.

The Small Business Administration will send you a free copy of its booklet, *Clipping Service*, which will provide you with more details about this type of enterprise.

WRITING FOR MAGAZINES AND NEWSPAPERS

Ever since the day they were first exposed to Hemingway, many people have wanted to be writers. For most of them, though, that goal never develops into anything more than a dream.

But if you believe that you possess some writing talent, and if you have perseverance, you can work at home as a freelance writer, and possibly earn over $20,000 a year.

Find yourself a quiet place in the house where you can write each day, and familiarize yourself with magazines that you might want to write for. What type of articles do they print? What length are they? What writing styles do they seem to prefer?

Then think of article ideas that might be appropriate for various magazines. For example, maybe *McCall's* might be interested in an article on how its readers can analyze nursing homes in their community. *Parent's Magazine* may find an article on childhood nightmares of interest. *Money* might be willing to print an article on how to buy a movie camera.

Find the name of the magazine's editor in the staff box, and send him a letter, explaining your article idea, and asking if it sounds of interest to him. Enclose a self-addressed stamped envelope for his reply. If he responds positively, write the article and if it's purchased, you can proudly tell your friends that, yes, you really are a writer now.

Read the various writer's magazines (*The Writer, Writer's Digest*), which will advise you on the types of articles that magazines may want at any particular time. Writing takes great discipline, so decide that you're going to write a certain number of hours each day—and do it. Once it becomes a habit, it won't seem nearly as difficult as it did when you first began.

LAUNCHING A BABY-SITTING ENTERPRISE

Phyllis O. has always been well-known throughout her neighborhood for two qualities—her dependability and her love of children. Thus, it wasn't surprising when she and her daughter started their own home baby-sitting business, and soon had neighbors flocking to them with their children. They now care for as many as 25 youngsters a day, make an income of $1500 a month, and enjoy every moment of it.

More mothers are working now than ever before, as a means of personal fulfillment, or out of economic necessity. In fact, about half of America's mothers with children under 18 have jobs outside their homes. And thus the need for child care is skyrocketing.

Although caring for children may seem like an ideal type of job, first think it over carefully. Youngsters have endless energy, frequently make ear-shattering noises. Is that something you can tolerate five or six days a week?

If the answer is "yes," then take the steps necessary to establish your own baby-sitting service. First check with city and county agencies to see if a license is required in your community. You may also be required to have some basic first-aid knowledge, but otherwise, special training is rarely needed.

Once you've taken care of any legal demands, then analyze your home situation. You will need a large playroom (living room or garage) and a sizable backyard. You should also have some toys and other play equipment (swings and slides would be ideal), plus room for a cot for every youngster. If you have to fence your property, you can expect to pay $450 to $500 for a chain-link fence around a 120-square-foot yard.

To attract customers, rely on neighbors to help you with word-of-mouth advertising. Small ads in community newspapers can bring in customers as well, as can notices on bulletin boards in laundromats, supermarkets, and churches:

PHYLLIS' BABY-SITTING SERVICE
Days & Evenings—All Ages/Hot Meals
Call 397-1881

You can charge $3 to $7 for day-long care of a child of a working mother. If you're levying fees by the hour, you can charge $1 or $2 per hour. Prices for additional services can run as follows: Serving a meal—$1.50, Bathing a child—$.50, Holiday care (e.g., New Year's Eve)—$8 to $15 per night.

Make certain that you know how to contact the parents of the children in your care, in case of an emergency. Also, always have the phone numbers of nearby emergency services handy.

Incidentally, because day-care or baby-sitting services usually attract children from only the immediate surrounding area, make certain that there are plenty of young families in your vicinity. If there aren't, you'll find yourself with fewer customers than you had anticipated.

COOKING YOUR WAY TO SUCCESS

Almost everyone has a food specialty that he or she can cook in the kitchen. And in today's world of processed and frozen foods, delicacies can rarely be found in local markets. However, there are many people who would eagerly buy homemade foods, if they knew where or from whom they could purchase them. And in many towns across the country, individuals are selling their cakes, cookies, breads, jellies and jams.

First, decide what food you think has marketability. Then test it to make certain that it's not just a family prejudice that makes the item taste as good as it does to you. Take it to a church bazaar or a women's club, and offer free or very inexpensive samples of the dish. If it meets with a positive response, then you're on your way.

Your next step is to obtain a permit from your local health department. Such a permit is normally needed whenever you are involved in any type of food preparation for public consumption. Before you are issued the permit, you may have to show proof of your own good health.

Then bake a few of your items and find an outlet or two willing to sell them for you. The corner mom-and-pop grocery store may be open to the idea. So might bakeries, candy stores, coffee shops, and a ᴿariety of other businesses. The item that you're baking may help you determine what your best outlet is.

In addition to selling your specialty foods at local stores, perhaps you should consider one or more of the following:

— Form your own box-lunch business, in which you serve employees of nearby offices by delivering tasty dishes to them at the noon hour.

— If you're an expert at baking cakes, why not specialize in wedding cakes? When you notice an announcement in the newspaper of an engagement or impending wedding, contact the bride's family and ask if they would be interested in having you supply the cake. Show them photographs of other wedding cakes you have baked.

— Cater parties with special hors d'oeuvres or desserts, and make them as exotic as possible. Talk to a friend who is planning a large party, and offer your cooking services. If your delicacies are delicious, you might receive requests to cater other parties. Word-of mouth is your best selling tool.

How much should you charge for your home-cooked items? Well, the general guideline is to determine your cost (including ingredients, electricity, packaging supplies, and delivery) and then double it. Depending on the item and how complex the cooking process is, you may choose to triple it.

Incidentally, if you really are an extraordinary cook, another home business to consider is teaching the culinary art to neighbors. If you specialize in a particular type of cuisine—i.e., French, Chinese, etc.—all the better. Or perhaps you can teach low-calorie cooking, or cooking for diabetics or allergy sufferers. Ideally, you should have a roomy kitchen and extra utensils for your students.

Advertise your classes on bulletin boards in grocery stores. If you're teaching a group of three or four pupils, charge them about $5 each for a two-hour class. Plan your teaching in advance, complete with photocopied recipes that your students can take home with them.

TYPING AT HOME FOR A BIG INCOME

Amy M. retired from her secretarial job in her mid-fifties. She had worked all of her adult life, and looked forward to a "life of leisure" in her retirement.

But as with so many other creative and energetic people, her retirement became more of a bore than a joy. Only nine months after she had left work, she became so eager to do something constructive that she finally decided to start her own home business—The Speedy Typing Service.

Within a year, Amy was already earning almost $275 a week— more than she had ever made during any of her working days. Her office is her kitchen table, and her only investment has been the purchase of an IBM Selectric typewriter.

A home typing service can be a very satisfying, money-making venture. If you can type fast and accurately, and if you also have dedication and an aggressive drive to find customers, you can earn $800 to $1200 a month—or more.

To launch your own typing service, you'll definitely need a good typewriter. It should not only be one that you can type rapidly upon, but also one that produces a neat and clean typewritten image. That 30-year-old manual model that you've stored in the attic for the last decade or two will probably not suffice.

However, there's no need to invest in a new $500-$800 electric machine—at least not right away. Instead, why not rent one for a few months? You can rent an IBM Selectric for $35-$45 a month in most communities, and this fee can usually be applied to the purchase price if you eventually decide to buy it. In the meantime, you can become accustomed to the machine and decide if it has all the features you need. The full rental fee is tax-deductible, too.

You may also want to print up some business cards, giving your name, address and phone number, and the type of service you offer. The cards will cost between $10 and $12 for a quantity of 1000.

Then it's time to search for customers. Hand out your cards at business offices, clubs, churches, and college dormitories. Also, place them on bulletin boards at community centers. You can also run a classified ad (under the heading of "Situations Wanted") in your local newspaper.

You might try a direct-mail letter to businessmen in your community, too, explaining your service to them. Send out 100 letters (which will cost you $13 in postage at 13 cents per letter). If the response is good, send out 100 more and watch your client list grow.

How much should you charge? Typical rates are from 40 to 75 cents per double-spaced page. You can add 10 to 15 cents per page if you have to transcribe the material from a tape recorder. An additional five cents can be charged for each carbon.

MAKING PROFITS IN PET-SITTING

There are more than 30 million dogs in America, and almost half that many cats. When pet owners in your city go on vacation, their animals have to be cared for by someone—and it could be you.

Ruth M. makes $8000 a year pet-sitting—while running another business (a typing service) from her home as well. She discovered that by charging less to pet-sit than nearby kennels (her fee—$3 a day, plus the cost of food), she was able to attract customers rather easily.

For such a business to succeed, you must have the space to keep the animals, preferably a large backyard. You should build a fence around the yard to confine the animals. Also, be willing to spend some time with each animal, walking him and giving him a personal touch that kennels often don't.

Check with local authorities to see what guidelines you'll have to follow. Is there a special license you need? Are there zoning regulations that might affect whether you can start such a home business in your neighborhood?

Once you launch your business, tell local pet shop owners of your new service. You could even offer them a commission for every customer they send your way. You might also contact dog license bureaus, and obtain a list of names of dog owners. You can also run an ad in the local dog-club newsletter. A small ad in the Yellow Pages is another attention-getter.

When your pet-sitting business begins doing well, you might consider branching out into other related areas, like a dog-grooming business (bathing, brushing, haircuts, nail clipping, etc.). Obedience classes are another possibility.

MANAGING AN APARTMENT BUILDING

One of the most interesting ways to work at home is to manage an apartment building. If apartment living appeals to you, and you like meeting and working with (and for) your fellow tenants, then recent offers like these will probably appeal to you:

WANTED—APT. MANAGER
Manage 200-unit beautiful garden apartments.
$12,000 guaranteed salary, plus profit-sharing and
free apt. Experience preferred but not necessary.

MANAGER wanted for 84-unit deluxe
high-rise. $850 mo. + 2 bdrm. apt. + bonus.

Technically, of course, managing an apartment building is not running your own business. But if you can locate a managerial position that offers profit-sharing, you'll be paid more than your promised salary if you're a good salesman, and can keep the units in your building occupied. The harder you work, the more you'll make—just as with your own business.

Keep in mind that managing a large apartment complex is a full-time job. You will have to show vacant units to prospective tenants. You may have to do some gardening chores as well, plus handyman jobs like fixing faucet leaks or installing new locks. Ordinarily you won't be asked to do anything too complex (like installing new carpeting or doing major plumbing work), but you may still have many responsibilities around the building.

Check your local newspaper for ads for apartment managers. Although experience is often not necessary, you might consider enrolling in a correspondence course in apartment managing (which will probably cost about $50 to $80). You'll learn the intracies of bookkeeping, simple maintenance, and how to deal with your tenants.

CHAPTER 9

How to Launch Your Money-Making Business

Ask the typical successful small businessman to list the most memorable days of his life, and he'll probably include his wedding day, the days his children were born, and the day of his business' grand opening.

If you've never had your own business before, you're in for a pleasant surprise on opening day. It's a delightful experience to see something that you've dreamed about for years come to fruition. Like so many others before you, you'll want to frame the first dollar bill that your business ever makes.

SELECTING THE NAME

Well before opening day, you should choose the name for your business. As we discussed earlier in this book, a good name can be extremely important to a new business' success. If it's descriptive and easy to remember—like Michael's Furniture Co. instead of Willow Interior Systems, Inc.—your chances of attracting and keeping customers is greater.

The name you select should be appropriate not only for the products you're selling now, but for those you may decide to add to your stock in several months or years. Perhaps you recall the problems Hotpoint had when it decided to market appliances other than stoves. The company's name was quite appropriate when it was selling ranges, but when it began marketing refrigerators as well, the public could not quite believe that a firm with the name of *Hot*point could manufacture and sell high-quality cooling appliances as well. Eventually, millions of dollars had to be spent on advertising to convince the public otherwise.

Of course, the small businessman can't afford such an enormous advertising budget. Thus, it's better to initially select a name that takes into account the future as well as the present. If your new store is specializing in outdoor rattan furniture, with the possibility of branching out into other types of outdoor furniture, it's better to name your business The Patio Shop rather than The Rattan Shop.

LEGALLY ASSUMING A NAME

Before opening day, fulfill any legal requirements you might have in terms of securing the name you have chosen. In most states, if you choose a fictitious name, you have to register it at the county clerk's office. The procedure is simple, requiring you to fill out a brief form, indicating the name of your small business, and the name(s) and home address(es) of the owner(s). There is usually a nominal fee levied for the filing procedure, of about $5 to $20, depending on the county. The purpose of this registration is to protect consumers against possible fraud, making it possible for them to trace the owner of a company if some illegal practice should occur.

USING ATTENTION-GETTERS

Attracting those very first customers during opening week is one of the most difficult tasks for a small businessman. How do you lure consumers away from the competition, making them *your* regular customers rather than *theirs*?

Ellen F. solved that problem in a rather unique way. In her middle years, she left her job as a medical office receptionist and started her own gift shop. The name she chose for her business, The Gift Gallery, was appropriate, but certainly not a "grabber" that would instantly fill her store with customers. But then she decided to stock and promote a gimmick item—a "square egg" maker. She had read about this device in a trade magazine, bought several dozen of them at wholesale, and had them on hand for opening day.

In the week before her grand opening, Ellen put signs on her storefront window, inviting people to drop in to see this novelty item, which compresses peeled hard-boiled eggs into a square shape. She promised to give five of them away in a drawing to be held that first afternoon.

Word-of-mouth traveled fast, and The Gift Gallery was filled with customers within hours of its opening. People were drawn in to look at the square egg maker, and while they were there, they did some other shopping as well. For Ellen, a gimmick payed off in a big way for her grand opening.

FINDING AN UNUSUAL ITEM

Certainly Ellen had the right idea. No matter what the competition is, if you can offer consumers something that your competitors don't, then you've already placed yourself a step ahead of them.

For instance, let's assume that you're thinking about opening up a restaurant/bar. This is probably one of the toughest small businesses to launch, because of the intense competition. Still, if you're able to cook your pizza in a way no one else does, or if your tropical drinks are the most unusual in town, then you've found a way to pull customers in.

However, you may not want to settle for just the uniqueness of your food and drink as a lure for potential customers. So how about installing a projector which, when hooked up to a TV set, projects the TV image onto a wall or a screen in a width up to six feet? You could put this device in your bar, and use it for sporting events or other widely viewed programs. Many people would rather watch a football game on a large screen with a roomful of people, instead of viewing it at home by themselves.

You can buy kits which will allow you to project such TV images. Some sell for as little as $16; others for only $60. This is an investment that may make your business boom from opening day.

A BUSINESS WITHOUT COMPETITION

The dream of every small businessman is to launch a business promoting a product that he—and only he—is selling. The best way to have customers waiting for you to open your doors at your grand opening is to have a totally unique product.

Of course, unless you're an inventor yourself, it's unlikely that you'll have the opportunity to sell items that no one else is selling. Still, if you're a bit ingenious and you study the marketplace carefully, you may come up with a business idea in which you will have only minimal competition.

How Howard S. Turned His Hobby into a Business

Let's say, for instance, that you are interested in automobiles. That was the case with Howard S., who enjoyed not only new cars, but antique ones as well. He owned a 1929 Ford model "A" Tudor sedan, which he treated like a child, as well as a more modern Toyota sedan, which he used for everyday driving.

Howard belonged to an antique car club, and one day while discussing old automobiles with some friends, he began thinking about starting a business that would "remanufacture" cars—that is, restore cars that are many years past their prime to operating condition. Howard lived in a big city, but even so, there was only one other such business in town, and that one remanufactured only Mercedes-Benz models. Howard's potential for success was definitely bright.

Within six months, he had launched British Classics Ltd. He specialized in restoring old cars originally manufactured in England, including Bentleys, Jaguars, Rolls Royces, Morgans, Triumphs, MGs, and Metros. He hired an experienced mechanic and an equally experienced auto body repairman. And although it's an expensive process to put old cars into excellent condition, there are many auto collectors willing to pay high prices for them.

British Classics Ltd. is now one of the most successful businesses of its kind in the country. Similar types of enterprises in other parts of the U.S. are doing equally well.

CREATING THE RIGHT GIMMICK

The secret to success, then, is to find a way to offer something out-of-the-ordinary on opening day. And if what you're selling is quite common, devise a way to present it in an unusual way. If you're selling hamburgers, for example, you can serve them on unusual buns. If you're selling roast beef or cheese sandwiches, give them unusual names (for example, use names of celebrities, calling sandwiches the Kirk Douglas, the Burt Lancaster, the Elizabeth

Taylor), and you'll find that some customers will be attracted out of curiosity.

THE PROPER STORE-FRONT APPEARANCE

During the first few days and weeks that you're open for business, you're going to depend greatly on "walk-in" customers. They will decide whether to enter your store or not based on its appearance from the street. So it's very important to capture the attention of passers-by, and lure them inside.

Take as much care in selecting the signs for the front of your store as in choosing your inventory. Without customers, your inventory isn't going to mean much. And the proper signs can bring in those consumers as quickly as anything else. Artful designs can attract attention, and get people talking about your store. Consider using something like supergraphics, carved wood or stained glass for your signs.

Window displays are also critical in catching customers' eyes. They present the best impression when they are original, clean and timely. (Don't leave a Valentine's Day display in the window through March.)

Consider the viewpoint of Myra G., who operates a successful plant shop. "The store window is the first contact that a customer has with my store," she says. "So what I try to do is reflect in my windows the quality of the merchandise inside. From the day I opened, I've put only my nicest plants in the window—and certainly none that were starting to wilt. I get the window-shoppers into my store by showing them the best I have to offer in as attractive a setting as possible."

In a plant store, window displays are changed frequently, as the greenery is sold and replaced with others. But even if you're in a business that does not sell a rapid turnover item like plants, never keep the same window display up for too long. That display that you have up on opening day should be replaced after a couple of weeks. Passers-by are always looking for something new, and they'll stop looking if your window displays never change. Ideally, a good window display will tell the potential customer: "Here is your chance to buy this product that you need or want."

AN ATTRACTIVE STORE INTERIOR

Once inside, the customer can be encouraged to browse awhile by an appealing interior. Try to make the decor fit the type of merchandise you are selling. For instance, if you're opening up a health food store, you probably want your interior to have as "natural" an appearance as possible, so you might use wood shelves and paneled walls to enhance this look. However, it might instead be appropriate for a health food store to have white walls and stainless steel counters, giving the feeling of cleanliness and good health. The decision is yours.

How Myra G. Put "Atmosphere" into Her Shop

When Myra G. started her plant shop, she attempted to create a tropical atmosphere in her store. She purchased a mechanical waterfall, which not only gave the store the feeling she wanted, but which also made just enough noise to block out the sounds of the automobiles on the street outside. She also played a radio in her store constantly, always tuned to a classical music station that seemed to relax and soothe the customers—and maybe even the plants.

No matter what type of business you have, it's wise to arrange your merchandise for opening day in such a way as to enhance your chances for impulse buying. Put items that you think will sell well adjacent to products that you're not quite so sure of. Half of the battle is just getting customers to see the product. If they don't see it—if it's displayed inconspicuously—then don't count on it selling well.

Frequently, displays supplied by manufacturers can help sales. Usually, these displays are designed to exhibit products in the best possible manner. Everyone from consumers to psychologists have been consulted in their design, and it's no coincidence that they can significantly help sales.

Incidentally, before your grand opening, make certain that the store is well-prepared in every way. For instance, is it well-lighted? Unless your store is bright in every alcove and nook, your first customers may feel more alienated than comfortable being in your shop.

Also, try to anticipate any problems that may arise in those first few days. A plant shop, for instance, will usually have wet floors because of constant watering and misting of the greenery. Don't wait until a customer slips and injures himself before you try to counteract that problem. Straw matting or other types of skid-resistant material on the floor can reduce the hazard and avoid a real tragedy.

When designing your store's exterior and interior, one of your best sources of information is trade magazines. Look through back issues available at the public library for ideas. You should also consider joining the trade association in your field. Check the *Encyclopedia of Associations,* available at the library, for the name and address of the trade organization in your field. There almost certainly is one, and it can provide you with some valuable advice on getting your business through those eventful first few weeks and months.

TIMING YOUR OPENING

Whenever possible, you should plan your grand opening for the most advantageous time of the year. For instance, it would be much wiser to launch your ice cream shop at the beginning of summer rather than at the start of winter. Likewise, a bridal shop has a much better chance of getting off to a good start if it opens in time for June weddings, rather than waiting until later in the year.

John Y. planned the opening of his bookstore to coincide with the Christmas season (which is also a good time to open many other types of businesses as well). His store, called The Book Mark, had its grand opening the Saturday after Thanksgiving, and was well-stocked for the Christmas rush.

"I had originally planned to open up the store in August," says John. "But I did some research, wrote a few letters, and talked to some other bookstore owners, and found out that the worst time of the year for book sales is during the hot summer months," says John.

"So I decided to wait a few extra months. Looking back, it would have been rather depressing to open up the store in August and have to wait until December to get the first big rush of customers."

Now, on the wall of his office, John has a chart that gives a month-by-month breakdown of what to expect in terms of sales. He compiled this information in the weeks preceding his own grand opening. No matter what type of business you operate, you should develop a chart similar to it, in order to help your own planning.

THE BOOKSELLER'S YEAR

January: A busy month; many gift certificates are used; heavily promoted sale books and remainders.

February: Quiet month; use time to take a thorough inventory, meet with publishers' representatives and return books that aren't selling; hold sale tying in with Valentine's Day.

March: Same as February.

April: Business improves; new titles come into the store; customers increase in number with spring vacations and buying for the Easter holidays.

May: Mother's Day; gear displays around this holiday, with emphasis on gift editions and art books.

June: Another good month, with graduations, weddings and Father's Day; display appropriate books prominently (e.g., dictionaries, post-wedding planning books, sports books).

July: Slow month; begin plans for ordering books for Christmas season.

August: Another slow month; continue planning for the fall and winter.

September: Good month; back-to-school time enhances sales of encyclopedias, dictionaries and textbooks.

October: Expect some Halloween-related sales; begin organizing store for Christmas, and making room for the new books that will soon be arriving.

November: Good month; Thanksgiving and pre-Christmas buying will enhance sales; hire and train help for Christmas; prepare window displays for Christmas.

December: The month when you'll earn 25 to 35 per cent of your annual profits; make certain you have plenty of gift wrapping paper; be willing to stay open extra long hours in the two weeks preceding Christmas.

HIRING COMPETENT EMPLOYEES

With many new businesses, there will be no need for you to hire any employees, at least during the first few weeks. You might be able to handle everything yourself—opening and closing the store, taking care of customers, ordering merchandise, and keeping your business records up-to-date.

However, even if you're able to manage on your own for awhile, there will probably—and hopefully—come a time when you'll have to hire help to assist you in meeting the demands of your increased customer load. Even if your business is a one-man shop throughout most of the year, you still might find it necessary to hire an extra employee or two during the peak times of the year—i.e., the Christmas season for a gift shop, the summer months for a fast-food restaurant at the beach.

The first step is for you to decide clearly in your own mind what the employee's duties will be. Do you need a salesman, or someone to work the cash register, or a stock boy, a custodian, a bookkeeper, a typist, a file clerk, etc.? If you've defined in advance all of the responsibilities of your new employee, you'll then know exactly what qualifications to look for in the applicants you'll interview. Defining the duties of the job will also give you an idea of how much to pay this individual. If you're looking for a skilled and experienced person, be willing to pay competitive wages to get him or her.

ATTRACTING APPLICANTS

There are several approaches you can use to find potential employees. The local office of the state employment bureau will do its best to locate the right individual for the job. Most of these state agencies will prescreen applicants before sending them to you for an interview. The employment office personnel should also be able to give you some advice on what the going salary is for the type of employee you are seeking.

Private employment agencies can also be used to try to find the proper employee. However, these offices are used mostly by larger businesses, who can afford to pay the fee that is charged for this service. Still, they are experts at pre-screening potential employees, and their fee may be worth the time they will save you.

Probably the most frequently used technique is to buy a classified ad in the local newspaper, advertising your need for an employee. The ad does not need to be large in order to attract attention. Individuals who are looking for work read the small ads as well as the large ones. So to keep your costs to a minimum, be as concise as possible in your classified notice.

As a guide, here are some typical classified ads that found the right employee the first day they were published.

> **DRIVER—Office furn. Must know city well. Gd driving rec. Sal. open. Call 937-4938 11-3PM.**
>
> **COOK, breakfast, part-time. Experience necessary. $5 hour. Apply 756 E. Monroe St.**
>
> **CLERK TYPIST, one-girl office, light bookkeeping. 857-3922.**
>
> **SALESPERSON—Retail furniture store near airport. Evening hours and weekends. Call 9:30 a.m.-12 noon. 485-0098.**
>
> **SECRETARY needed by real estate co. Xlnt. typing & clerical skills. Light shorthand. Call 937-6647.**

FINDING MR. OR MS. RIGHT

Once the calls begin coming in, you should have a system planned which will allow you to interview these people without taking away time from your business day. Mildred W., who runs a dress shop, usually has some free time during the morning, so when potential employees called her, she would ask them to come by the following day before 12 noon. At that time, she had them fill out an application form, which she had obtained at a local stationery store, and she talked to each of them for a short while after the application had been completed. She found the saleswoman she needed this way, and her business didn't suffer at all during the interviewing process.

At the time of the interview, be prepared to tell the prospective employee what his salary will be, as well as any benefits you are willing or able to offer (health insurance, sick leaves, paid holidays). Clearly define for him or her what the working hours will be, and precisely what duties will be involved.

Then go over the application with the person, asking any appropriate questions that come to mind. For instance, why does he want or need the work? Will he be able to work overtime if necessary? What was his reason for leaving his previous job? Ask for references, and when you've narrowed your choices down to the top two or three, call the references that have been given. Hopefully, these references can vouch for the individual's responsibility and integrity, as well as tell you about any problems they're aware of with the person.

TRAINING YOUR NEW EMPLOYEE

Once you've hired the individual who will be working for you, take the time to train him properly to ensure that he'll handle his duties the way you want him to. If he's a sales clerk, he should be fully familiarized with your policy toward check cashing, refunds, discounts, gift certificates, and other matters. He should know as much as possible about the products he will be selling, including where and how they were manufactured, and the type of guarantee they carry. Always encourage your employees to ask questions about anything they are uncertain about.

If for any reason, the employee who you have hired simply does not do his job well, it's foolish to hang onto him too long. Once the individual has had ample opportunity to "learn the ropes," he should be fired if he is consistently incompetent. When it is clear that he has been hired for a job that he cannot handle, for the good of the business you can't afford to keep him working for you indefinitely.

For those employees who do well, let them know that you are pleased with their work. Give these individuals regular salary increases, and tell them that you're hiking their wages because you're happy with them.

HIRING RELATIVES

The problems that come with hiring and keeping good employees can be avoided if you're lucky enough to have family members available to help you get your business started. That was the case with John Y., the bookstore owner described earlier. His 19-year-old twin daughters became his first employees. So during the critical first few weeks that he was open for business, he did not have to worry about finding and hiring dependable help; they already lived right in his own house.

John's daughters spent many hours at his store after their college classes were over for the day. They helped him tally every book that was in stock, and make notes about ordering certain titles. They meticulously read trade publications like *Publisher's Weekly*, which he didn't have time to do during those initial hectic weeks. They were able to keep him abreast of the books that were best-sellers, as well as the titles that would probably be selling well in the near future because of planned advertising campaigns by the various publishers.

"I'd rather have the girls working for me than someone who I'm hiring cold," says John. "The girls have been enthusiastic about the business from the beginning. To them, it's more than a job. Since it's their father's store, they have a stake in seeing it succeed. They're more likely to go out of their way to please customers than would someone whose main interest is his paycheck at the end of the week."

REFLECTING BACK ON THE GRAND OPENING

No matter how your new business does during the first few days and weeks, keep things in perspective. If you've done better than you ever imagined you would, you still have the task of attracting new customers and keeping those that you've already acquired. If things haven't gone as well as you had hoped, then accept the challenge of pursuing those consumers who have not yet heard about your store.

Whatever has happened in the initial days after you open your doors, you will almost certainly feel a real sense of excitement for some weeks to come. After all, you finally have your own new business. And as you iron out the kinks in the subsequent weeks and months, it will undoubtedly only become more exciting.

CHAPTER 10

Conquering the Business Side of Your Money-Making Enterprise

As your small business expands into a bigger one, you will thoroughly enjoy watching it grow. However, in order for it to thrive over the long term, you will have to establish an efficient record-keeping system and keep it up-to-date.

Maintaining these business records is an essential part of every business. Although it may seem tedious, in its own way, it is as important as customer relations or any other facet of your enterprise. Without a proper bookkeeping system, it will be nearly impossible to keep track of the financial progress that you're making.

Experts say that the most serious management mistake that a small businessman can make is to keep incomplete or inaccurate financial records. A weak accounting system can harm almost every aspect of your business—from sales to inventory control to taxes.

BOOKKEEPING INGREDIENTS

A good record-keeping system can take many directions. The type of system you establish should be one with which you feel comfortable. But no matter what shape your plan takes, the Small Business Administration suggests that it possess all of the following qualities:

1. Simple to use.
2. Easy to understand.
3. Dependable.
4. Accurate.
5. Enduring.
6. Able to furnish information on a timely basis.

159

ORGANIZING YOUR RECORDS

Walk up and down the aisles of a large stationery store, and you'll find all the forms you need to set up a complete record-keeping system. As the differences between one form and another will indicate, there are many ways to record the same information. Precisely how you do it is up to you. But there are certain records that are essential.

For instance, you must keep a *daily summary* of cash receipts, based upon your cash register tapes, sales receipts and charge account slips. You also need an *expense ledger*, where you can tabulate all the money being spent, both cash and checks, for rent, payroll, accounts payable, etc. (Don't overlook keeping track of how you spend petty cash.)

An *inventory purchase journal* should also be maintained, which will keep a tally on the shipments you receive, your accounts payable, and the cash you have available for purchases in the upcoming weeks and months. If you have other people working for you, an *employee compensation record* should be used to list wages and deductions that have been withheld.

Maintaining a Ledger

At the end of each month, your data on income and expenses should be totaled, and posted in a permanent *ledger*. At a glance, this ledger will provide you with a perspective of your monthly, quarterly and annual income and operating expenses. The expenses should be categorized by item, to allow you to compare this month's (or year's) outlay to that of last month (or year). Only then can you get some sense of how your business is progressing.

It would also be wise to maintain a running *balance sheet* of your business' total assets and liabilities. Your assets will include the money in your business' checking account, the inventory on hand, the equipment you own, and your accounts receivable. Liabilities would include any money you owe to lenders and wholesalers. The net worth of your business is the difference between your assets and liabilities.

SOME TIPS TO BETTER RECORD-KEEPING

As the months go by, you'll develop your own techniques for keeping records. You will create your own particular way of organizing and filing. By all means, use the system that works best for you, as long as it is complete and meets the six SBA ingredients described above.

No matter what system you finally employ, there are some basic guidelines which, if followed, will ensure that your record-keeping is thorough. For instance:

—Every one of your invoices, statements, purchase orders and checks should be numbered sequentially. If you are using standard printed forms that are numberless, write the appropriate number in the upper right corner as you use it.

—All of your transactions should be dated. Like numbering, this is a method of keeping your records organized, and a good reference point from which to trace any problems that might occur.

—Each transaction should be photocopied if a carbon copy has not already been made of it. This copy should be filed separately from the original. For instance, if the original is filed by the customer's last name, then the copy can be filed by date, or by the type of item purchased. You will not only have a system of cross-reference this way, but if a particular form becomes misplaced, you will also have another copy of it.

—Your important papers can be filed in anything from shoe boxes to the most expensive file cabinets. But no matter what you employ, your system should be kept up-to-date, and organizational dividers should be strategically placed so that you can locate a particular item with no trouble.

Using a Calendar

—Have a calendar hanging by your desk, which is large enough to make notes on. You should mark in advance the dates that particular merchandise will have to be ordered, and the dates on which it is to be delivered. Unless you keep track of these matters in an organized way, ordering and delivery dates may pass without your even realizing it. If a delivery doesn't arrive on the date promised, you should be on the phone immediately finding out why.

OTHER TYPES OF RECORDS

In addition to the general kinds of records described above, almost every type of business has need for some other records. Ice cream shops, for instance, often keep a file of the birthdays of their regular customers. A few days before each birthday, a postcard is sent out to the customer, inviting him to come in for a free cone or drink. This promotional technique is an excellent method of creating good will among the public, but it requires a well-organized filing system.

Mark P.'s Birthday Greetings System

"I ask customers to fill out a 3 × 5 card, with their name, address and phone number on it," says Mark P., who operates an ice cream parlor in the West. "I file these cards chronologically according to birthdate, and on the first day of each month, I pull out the cards for that month, and have my wife send out the notices to everyone celebrating a birthday that month. We also glance ahead to the next month, to see if there's someone with a birthday on the first few days of that month. If there is, we send them out a card as well, so they get it in plenty of time."

Other businesses use other types of specialized record-keeping systems. For instance, pet grooming shops usually maintain files on their customers and their pets. A common system is to use a separate file card for each customer, making note of his name, address, phone number, and the name and type of pet (including sex, breed, and color). When a customer returns to the shop with his pet for grooming, the store owner can look at the file card, on which is also indicated the date of the last appointment, any particular problems or instructions that accompanied that grooming, and the fee that was charged.

THE PROPER METHOD OF HANDLING OF CASH

Many small businessmen are quite successful in establishing a record-keeping system. Most devise efficient methods of filing invoices, receipts, and the many other types of papers that are used in their business. But the one area in which many businesses have more problems than any other is in handling cash and checks. At month's end, there is often a descrepancy between what the record books say and the way the checking account balance reads.

Frankly, this should never happen. And there are some concrete steps you can take to eliminate problems in this area. The following points should all become part of your everyday working procedures:

1. If you have employees who handle cash and securities, have them bonded. This is a relatively inexpensive procedure, and it will serve to dissuade them from any dishonest action.

2. Your business' securities should be locked in a safe deposit vault. If you don't do so, and they are misplaced, you will have caused yourself much inconvenience.

3. Each day's cash receipts should be deposited in the bank as soon as possible. With the crime rate being what it is, it's foolish to leave large amounts of cash stored in a desk drawer, or even in a safe in your own office.

4. Avoid writing out checks to "cash," or signing checks without also indicating the amount and the party to whom they are directed. A signed bank check sitting atop a desk or in a drawer is an invitation to anyone with dishonest thoughts.

5. If you send out large amounts of mail, use a postage meter rather than stamps. With a meter, you can keep better track of your mailing costs, and there is less risk of misuse of postage than with stamps.

6. Keep close control over your petty cash fund. Use it only to pay small expenditures, and limit it to a certain amount each week. Don't add extra money to your petty cash drawer without making a note of it. In too many businesses, petty cash money appears and disappears without any record of where it has come from and where it has gone.

7. You should examine your accounts payable carefully and frequently. The bills you receive from your suppliers should be checked against the vouchers given to you at the time of delivery. They sometimes don't agree, and businessmen end up paying more money than they actually owe.

SHOULD YOU OFFER CREDIT?

The mere thought of extending credit to customers is often enough to make the average businessman shudder. The additional paperwork alone has turned some store owners away from the concept altogether.

"I run a very small stationery store," says Margery W. "I never intended to have any large business accounts. To do so, I'd need a lot more floor and storage space, and I'd have to spend a lot more time at the job. I'm getting close to retirement, and I started this store with the hopes that I wouldn't have to work as hard as I had earlier in life. I want to make a comfortable living, but I want to enjoy myself as much as possible, too."

Most of Margery's customers are high school and college students, who purchase their stationery supplies from her, and housewives who buy items like photo albums, greeting cards, and address books. "No individual purchase is really for that much money," she says. "If people were spending $30 to $40 at a time, then I might consider offering credit as a convenience to them. But I bet I haven't heard more than a complaint or two in the last year about the fact that I will accept only cash."

When making your decision about whether or not to offer credit, keep in mind that there are some consumers who like it, and will buy only at stores that make charge accounts available. Of course, if you operate a very small store like Margery's, a charge service may not be necessary. But in many other cases, one of the best methods of building up a loyal clientele is to provide a convenient form of credit. Customers who use credit tend to shop more often than those who don't, and they make larger purchases, too.

Using Credit Cards

Several methods can be used to handle consumer credit. Probably the simplest way is to honor bank charge cards like Bankamericard and MasterCharge, or travel and entertainment credit cards like American Express, Carte Blanche and Diners Club. By accepting these cards in your store, you relieve yourself of the laborious chore of verifying credit reliability among your customers. You are also not responsible for billing and collecting, and there is no risk of ever incurring losses because of unpaid credit. These credit card companies will charge you a fee for their service, which is usually dependent upon your average monthly charge sales. The fee averages about three percent.

Most small businessmen do not establish their own independent charge accounts until they have several shops, or until they have enough personnel to handle the complex paperwork that accompanies any personal credit service. Keep in mind, though, that most store owners find that the headaches involved with their own credit system often outweigh any benefits that may accrue from it. The bank or T&E credit cards are probably your best credit alternative.

ASSESSING YOUR INSURANCE NEEDS

If you don't already have an insurance broker whom you have used in the past and are pleased with, then find one. Opening a small business without the proper insurance is almost suicidal. A good insurance agent will advise you as to the best kinds of insurance for your particular business. He will also consult with you periodically in the upcoming years and months as to how your insurance needs change with time.

To find a good insurance broker, don't rely on playing roulette with the phone book. Ask for personal referrals from friends and business associates. Some agents and brokers are informed and honest; others are ignorant about the product they sell, and are more interested in having you buy as much insurance as possible rather than buying only the insurance that you need.

Here are the various types of insurance which you should discuss with the agent or broker with whom you finally decided to do business:

—**Fire insurance** that will cover damage to the building, the equipment and the inventory you have. It should protect against damage caused not only by fire, but also smoke, windstorms, tornadoes, explosions, riots, and aircraft. Ask your agent to periodically reevaluate this coverage with you, to make certain that you are always insured to the full value of these assets.

—**Liability insurance** that will cover you against any losses caused by claims of bodily injury or property damage connected with your business. This would protect you if a customer injures himself in a fall in your store, or if the awning in front of your shop collapses on top of a pedestrian.

—**Crime insurance** that will protect you against burglary and robbery, as well as vandalism and employee theft.

—**Automobile insurance** for any business-owned vehicles—e.g., delivery trucks. You should cover yourself for both collision and public liability.

—**Business interruption insurance**, which will reimburse you for any money you have lost during a brief stop in normal business operations due to serious illness or fire.

—**Fidelity bonds**, which are placed on employees who have access to your business' funds. With this kind of protection, you won't have to worry about loss from embezzlement.

—**Workmen's compensation insurance**, which is required by law to cover medical costs and loss of pay from job-related injuries.

—**Health insurance**, which if you have several employees, can usually be purchased in a group package at substantial discount over buying one or more individual policies. Although the cost of health insurance for your employees may be difficult to justify when you're trying to get a new business started, you will almost certainly have to eventually offer such coverage in order to keep your best workers. If you can't afford to assume the entire cost of the insurance yourself, be willing to share the cost with each individual employee, or at least make the relatively inexpensive group rates available to them if they want to purchase the coverage on their own.

MAKING THE MOST OF MAIL ORDER

A mail-order small business can be a most successful venture. However, more than in most other types of businesses, mail order requires meticulous record-keeping procedures. Every step in the mail-order process involves paperwork in some form. So although success in this kind of endeavor requires foremost a very saleable product, unless you also are organized and thorough in the paperwork that's necessary, you're not going to cash in on the large profits that are possible.

How Bertram K. Caught Up on His Record-Keeping

"About three years ago I had a growing mail-order business going," recalls Bertram K., who went into business for himself for the first time in his middle years. "I was selling just one product—iron-on fabric decals. Business was good, and I was doing OK in keeping my book work up to date.

"Eventually I added two additional products—antique photo kits and novelty T-shirts. In the first few weeks of getting these new products off the ground, I foolishly neglected my decal business for awhile. The mail piled up, I wasn't filling orders, I wasn't keeping track of the money coming in, and I stopped keeping a running list of my customers for future contact.

"Finally, I got my wife to help bail me out. We spent an entire weekend catching up on what I had let lapse. We processed all the unopened mail, and sent out the products that had been ordered. I brought all my logs and ledgers up to date."

Bertram K.'s story has a very happy ending. He has added still two more mail-order products in recent months—including redwood greenhouses—and his annual earnings are now exceeding $30,000. He has hired a part-time secretary, who helps Bertram keep his business operating efficiently. Needless to say, Bertram has vowed to never again let poor record-keeping—nor any other facet of his business—jeopardize his success as a small entrepreneur.

IS MAIL ORDER FOR YOU?

Mail order has experienced a dramatic increase in popularity in the past few years. Unusual products—a staple of mail order—are selling better than ever these days, as are more ordinary items that are not obtainable in certain smaller cities in the country.

Thousands of people of all ages and backgrounds are making attractive livings these days in the mail order industry. As with all other enterprises, you must be willing to expend the time and effort to make the business a success. But mail order is an ideal endeavor for someone who, because of health or age reasons, does not have the physical energy of a high school student anymore.

To prosper in mail order, you must follow some basic steps that are essential to the entire operation. First of all, you need a mailing address, which can be your office, your home or a post office box. If possible, use a street address rather than a P.O. box, since many people think that a street address reflects stability in a company. However, there are nevertheless thousands of mail-order businesses that are flourishing using P.O. addresses.

Omitting Your Street Address

If you live in a small town where you actually know the local postmaster personally, ask him if arrangements can be made so the only mailing address you need is your name and the name of your town—without any street address: e.g., Thomas Stephens, McCamey, Tex.; or Mail Products, Mankato, Kan. Such a mailing format is possible if the postmaster will agree to it. Not only is it somewhat prestigious to have your mailing address appear that way, but it will help avoid any mistakes your customers might make in writing out your street address.

ANALYZING YOUR MAIL ORDER MARKET

Your potential market for mail order should be studied as carefully as if you were opening a store-front business. Most buyers of mail-order products fall into distinct categories: (a) people who enjoy novelty items, (b) those who are pursuing a hobby, (c) those who buy via mail because of convenience, and (d) those on the lookout for bargains.

When you're searching for one or more products to sell to them, keep their desires in mind. Don't bother with items that are universally available. Try to find the out-of-the-ordinary products to sell, which are often listed in trade magazines. Also contact gift manufacturers and wholesalers who are listed in the Yellow Pages, and inquire about the various products that they may be able to supply you with.

Perhaps a local craftsman in your community can provide you with special items you can sell.

FIVE IMPORTANT PRODUCT QUALITIES

Whatever product you finally decide upon, be sure that it meets all of the five qualities printed below. If it is lacking in even one of them, think twice before investing your time and energy into it.

1. It should not already be offered by a major mail order house (unless you are able to sell it for substantially less money than these competitors).
2. It should be an odd, extraordinary, novelty or specialty item.
3. It should be able to sell itself through printed advertisements. Products like dresses or suits are normally difficult to sell through the mails, because buyers usually feel better trying on these types of items. But less personalized items can be big mail-order sellers.
4. It must lend itself to repeat sales. Personalized return-address labels, for example, can be ordered and reordered indefinitely by the same individual for as long as he continues to send letters. So can health and beauty aids, auto accessories, pet products, and party items. Try to avoid thinking in terms of just a single sale to any one person.
5. Its sale must not violate any federal, state or local regulations. Current laws governing the sale of products like food, cosmetics and drug items can be obtained from the U.S. Food and Drug Administration, Washington, D.C. 20204.

SETTING A SALE PRICE

Putting a price on a mail-order product is not a simple matter. But there are some general guidelines that you can follow. For instance, for inexpensive items that you can buy at wholesale for a dollar or less, a mark-up of about 250 percent is acceptable. As the wholesale price increases, the mark-up should decrease. So an item that costs you $2.50 or $3 might warrant a 100 percent mark-up. A product with a $5 wholesale price could be sold for 75 percent over cost.

When setting your price, take into consideration what your advertising expenses are likely to be. The way that the public will learn of your product is through the media, and purchasing advertising space is certainly not cheap. Still, keep in mind that a good ad campaign will more than pay for itself, bring in enough customers to cover the cost of the ads, plus earn you a handsome profit as well.

AN ADVERTISEMENT THAT WORKS

Louise S. is operating her own successful mail-order business today. Although she sells several items, the most popular one is a metal watchband calendar that attaches to the wristband of a standard-size men's leather band. She credits her advertising campaign for the large sales of this item.

Louise's ad, which she runs in various newspapers across the country, is not large nor particularly clever. But it includes a clear, close-up photograph of the calendar, affixed to a watchband. The ad copy itself reads:

WATCHBAND CALENDAR

Never again will you have to guess at the date when you have this easy-to-read, large-print calendar attached to your men's watchband. The calendar is available in silver or gold. Sundays and holidays are printed in red. For $1.85, you'll receive 12 separate calendars, one for each of 12 months. Specify the month you would like your 12-month series to start. Send check or M.O. to CALENDAR PRODUCTS, Corsicana, TX.

When Louise receives responses, she fills the orders the same day, making a record of the full name and address of the buyer, the check or money order number with which payment was made, and the calendar months that were sent to that individual (e.g., June 1977 to May 1978). Then several months later, as that calendar year is running out, she mails a little notice to the buyer, with an invitation to purchase the next series of 12 months. To Louise, this record-keeping system is critical to getting repeat customers, who are an important part of her overall success.

"I feel very responsible to the customers who patronize me," says Louise. "I am determined to give them a good product and good service. And I've found by doing so, they are eager to do business with me again. The new customers I receive every week are paying the bills for me; the repeaters are the ones who are making me richer than I've ever been before."

CHAPTER 11

The Money-Making Way
to Attract Customers

No matter how successful your business is, you should never be content with the number of customers you have. There's always an opportunity to attract even more. And the larger your clientele, the greater your potential for profits.

There are many ways to attract new customers, and some of them have already been discussed earlier in this book. All of those techniques that you used to lure consumers into your store during its opening days can continue to be applied indefinitely.

Of course, your best method of luring customers into your fold as the months go by is to offer them a desirable product or service at a reasonable price. No matter how clever the name of your store, how good the location, or how creatively designed your window displays, consumers are going to stay away unless the products you sell are just as attractive.

TAKING OVER AN ESTABLISHED STRUCTURE

When Stanley R. opened up his new restaurant, he wanted people to notice it immediately. He not only hoped that passers-by would see it, but he wanted the restaurant to be so unusual that they would feel almost compelled to stop in.

Creating a Really Unusual Restaurant

"There's so many other restaurants in this town that I knew I'd have to do something out of the ordinary to get my share of the customers right away," he says. "So I bought three old railroad cars, which were headed for a salvage yard and were being sold for almost nothing. I had the interiors renovated, the seats removed, new carpeting put in, and tables and chairs added. The exteriors were painted to

175

give them a brand-new appearance. The railroad cars then were connected—and they became my restaurant."

Frankly, Stanley's restaurant became the talk of the city. The local newspaper ran a story on it before it opened, and then again afterward. Reservations and diners poured in the first few days, and the rush of customers has never ended. Once the novelty of the restaurant wore off, the good quality of the food brought people back repeatedly.

In recent years, innovative businessmen have turned railroad cars, boats, abandoned train stations and even a spacious bank vault into the sites for their restaurants. Other entrepreneurs in other types of business have moved into more traditional structures, but have dramatically changed the building's image or appearance with major renovations.

Using Vacated Buildings

Yes, retailers have found that taking over a deserted storefront can have real advantages. For instance, when Daylin Inc. closed its 108 stores in 1975, many small businessmen quickly moved in to take over the vacated store space. The same thing happened when W.T. Grant & Co. shut down its 66 stores. These major retail chains had chosen their sites carefully, and although they were forced to close because of poor management, the store locations were still attractive—and were often available for bargain-basement prices.

HOW A MINI-MALL ATTRACTS CUSTOMERS

The mini-mall is a relatively new concept in American small business operations. But if one exists in your town, you should examine the possibility of launching your business in it.

The mini-mall concept is ideal for an individual who wants to open a full-fledged enterprise with strong consumer appeal, and yet who desires to work less than a 40-hour week. The mini-mall typically consists of a group of small shops that operate under a common roof. For instance, the mini-mall in McKeesport, Pa. has 100 separate shops. In the mini-mall in Willingboro, N.J., there are 100 vendors.

Patterns of Mini-Mall Operation

Traditionally, mini-malls are open a far less number of hours than is typical in the business world. The American Village mini-mall in Willingboro is open for business only 24 hours a week—Thursday and Friday nights and all day Saturday and Sunday.

"As far as I can tell, the mini-mall is just perfect for the small businesswoman like me," comments Rachael G., who has operated her own fabric shop since 1975. "There is a tremendous amount of foot traffic in the mall, and so there has been no problem at all attracting customers. Also, because the store is open only four days a week, for a total of only 24 hours, I still have a lot of time to spend at home with my family. Neither I nor they think that I've neglected them at all."

Rachel also notes that many of her fellow entrepreneurs in the mini-mall are nearing retirement age, or have already reached it. "Some of them tell me that they might have already retired were it not for the mini-mall concept," she says. "Here they can work only four days a week, and still be assured that they're going to attract enough customers on that part-time basis. In any other location, they'd probably have to stay open six or seven days a week to get the same number of patrons.

SUCCEEDING WITHOUT A STOREFRONT

Although an attractive storefront in a highly traveled area can be an important factor in drawing customers, you can still make a success of your business without it. This is particularly true of a business whose customers never have to physically be on the premises. A good word-of-mouth campaign, well-placed advertising or an effective flyer inserted under automobile windshield wipers will find you customers even if you're upstairs in a small office building.

Taylor E. operates an aquarium-cleaning business, using as his headquarters nothing more than a small one-room office a block away from the town's business center. Since his maintenance business is handled entirely through house and office calls, he has no need at all for an attractive and conspicuously located store. He requires only a place to keep his equipment, and the tiny room he rents suffices nicely. Taylor has built up his route extremely well, and now earns nearly $20,000 a year after expenses.

Businesses Without Offices

Other small businesses have no need for *any* type of office at all, and still are able to attract a considerable number of customers. Consider the case of Sheila Y., who is a talented home decorator. Her working place is the houses of others, who hire her to solve their decorating problems.

Sheila has used various methods to find her customers, in lieu of not having an office along a busy street. She has made arrangements with several furniture stores to let her display her business cards on their sales counters. She has also made speeches to women's clubs and church groups, and through these appearances, has attracted customers. She has placed ads in local newspapers, too, which have been very effective.

MAKING GOOD USE OF ADVERTISING

Advertising is one of the most important money-making tools that any small businessman can use. The power of a good ad is overwhelming. Time after time, a store suffering from a scarcity of customers has been transformed into a thriving enterprise through advertising.

How Much You Should Spend on "Ads"

Almost every kind of business can benefit from advertising and promotion. Although the proportion of income spent on ads varies from one retail establishment to another, a healthy average is from 1½ percent to 3 percent. During the first year of operation, perhaps as much as 5 percent should be spent.

In general, the more money you allocate for advertising, the more your sales will increase. However, certain types of businesses usually require more ads than others to attain the same level of sales. A clothing store, for example, typically needs a higher turnover than an antique store, and thus must spend more on advertising. A business that offers many customer services (free delivery, attractive credit privileges, good exchange policy) generally necessitates less advertising than one that doesn't.

If your store is located in an out-of-the-way spot, you'll have to rely heavily on advertising to let people know that you exist. Also, whenever you begin offering a new product or service, you should temporarily increase your ad budget to get the word out. If you have a neighborhood store, you will probably only need to advertise in the local suburban newspaper; but if you're trying to attract customers from a very large area, you should be thinking of running more expensive ads in large, metropolitan papers.

ADVERTISING IN NEWSPAPERS

When small businessmen think of advertising, they should focus on newspapers—usually the suburban newspaper in their community. Their ads are relatively inexpensive, and reach a large number of people.

All papers offer two categories of ads—the display ads and the classifieds. The displays are more eye-catching, but they are also more expensive. To find out which will work best for you, consider running ads in both formats on different weeks.

Gene D. began an advertising campaign in the local newspaper when he opened up a tuxedo rental shop. The first week, he ran a small classified ad:

> **THE CUSTOM TUX SHOP. Rentals.**
> **All sizes. All colors. Compare**
> **our prices. Open Sunday. 9346**
> **Burton Ave. Call 671-5900.**

"I was pleased with the response," recalls Gene. "I had a few phone calls because of it, and some people who came into the store mentioned seeing the ad."

Classified vs. Display Advertising

After running the classified ad for a total of three consecutive weeks (at a cost of \$3.15 per week), Gene decided to run a larger, display ad, which cost him \$35 a week. The ad allowed him to say much more than the small classified ad did:

Come first to

THE CUSTOM TUX SHOP

The latest styles & colors:

—**Baggies**
—**Flairs**
—**Colored Shirts**

**All sizes & all colors for
men and boys.
Wedding Specialists.
Also see us for proms
(and student discounts).
Perfect Fit by Expert Tailors.
Compare our prices.
Ample Free Parking.
Open 7 days a week (½-day Sun.)
9346 Burton Ave.
671-5900**

"A lot of people read classifieds, but usually they do it only when they're looking for something specific, like a used car and an apartment to rent," analyzes Gene. "Some people saw my classified, but I know from the increase in customers that a lot more saw my display ad. Let's face it—I had to pay more money for the larger ads. But I've more than got back what I put in. I'm a firm believer in advertising now."

OTHER ADVERTISING OUTLETS

Although you will probably concentrate your advertising efforts on newspapers, at least be aware of the other media available to you. Advertising dollars can also be spent in local magazines, "shoppers" flyers, direct mail, billboards, telephone solicitations, radio and television.

There may be times when other outlets will work more to your advantage than newspapers, so keep them in mind. Don't ever allow yourself to become so narrow-minded as to think that since newspapers have worked for you in the past, only they can ever provide results for you in the future.

Unfortunately, expensive radio and TV ad rates are usually prohibitive for most small businessmen. Some retailers, though, are able to share these high TV and radio expenses with product manufacturers. For instance, a bookstore can often take advantage of cooperative advertising programs offered by publishers. Under these plans, a retailer can be reimbursed up to 75 per cent of his total advertising costs by submitting copies of advertisements which promote specific books published by that company. Similar types of arrangements are frequently tendered by manufacturers of products ranging from TV sets to refrigerators to toys to phonograph records.

WRITING AN EFFECTIVE AD

It's been said that advertising can sell anything—(remember the Pet Rock discussed earlier in this book?)—and there is certainly some truth to that. But also keep in mind that a well-written ad will be many times more effective than a poorly-written one. Yes, a bad ad may still bring some people into your store, but a good one will bring two, five or ten times as many.

Compare the following two ads which ran recently in the same big-city newspaper:

**The ears have it at
THE SOUND MACHINE!
We'll meet your every stereo need.
We've never been undersold.
Come in and hear for yourself.
(Address and phone here.)**

**STEVE'S STEREO
We sell a wide selection of stereo and quad components. We invite you to look and listen to our name brands like Marantz, Pioneer, Dual, Teac, and JBL. Big discounts**

**are made on used equipment, and credit is available.
Conveniently located.
Since 1967.
We encourage your comparison shopping.
(Address and phone here.)**

Which of these ads do you like better? Which would attract your patronage?

Advertising experts would pick the second one. True, the simplicity of the first one is a virtue, but it is really too simple. There are no specifics about exactly what type of products are being sold. A good ad should tell what the customer can expect when he enters your store, and that means saying more than "We'll meet your every stereo need." Also, the claim in the first ad that "We've never been undersold" is unrealistic; every store, even the biggest discount house in town, has been undersold by someone at one time or another. Ads shouldn't make claims that no one is going to believe.

Here, then, are five ingredients of a good ad. After you write your ads, be sure that they possess all of these qualities:

1. Simplicity (you can promote more than one item or make more than one sales pitch, but use your judgment to avoid putting *too* much into an ad).
2. Strength (attempt to show conviction and that you believe in yourself and your products).
3. Believability (extravagant claims tend to backfire rather than attract customers).
4. Quality (use proper grammar, and if your ad includes sketches or photos, they should be of a high caliber).
5. Restraint (show some honesty and modesty; you can appeal to readers without telling them that you and your store are the "Muhammad Ali" of the business world).

EVALUATING YOUR AD'S EFFECTIVENESS

When you're advertising, it's often easy to determine the potency of your campaign. If business had been slow, but it suddenly picks up after your ad runs, then the ad probably deserves most of the credit. Even if business is already good before the ad campaign, but customers suddenly begin asking for the specific product that you featured in the newspaper that week, then you know that people have read and reacted to what your ad has said.

Many store owners ask first-time customers what brought them in. Was it the ad in that week's newspaper? Or did the motivation come from elsewhere—word-of-mouth advertising, window displays or signs, the Yellow Pages, etc.? Also ask your regular customers whether they've seen the ads. If so, have the ads made them aware of some aspect of your business that they did not know before?

Sticking with an Ad That Works

If you seem to receive more negative feedback about your ads than positive, don't necessarily cancel them. Frequently, ads must run several times before they begin to make a real impact. In fact, once you have a well-written ad that says exactly what you want to say, you should commit yourself to stay with it over the long term. Repetition will increase knowledge of and interest in your store and/or products. The results may pleasantly surprise you if you stick with it.

After you've run several ad campaigns, you'll probably find that some were definitely more successful than others. There can be many reasons for this. Certainly the time that the ad was run can be responsible for the response it received. So can a number of other factors, including the message and how well it was conveyed, whether your slogans (if any) stuck to the point, and whether the illustrations used were appealing or offensive. With the passage of time, you'll become more skillful at analyzing your own ads, and writing more effective ones.

USING OTHER PROMOTIONAL TECHNIQUES

Paid advertisements can turn an average small business into an extraordinary one. But in order to cultivate as large a clientele as possible, you should also use certain other types of outlets available to you.

Free publicity, for instance, is often possible in the local newspapers, or on radio and TV. If you own a restaurant, a mention by a respected restaurant critic in a positive way can be worth more than a dozen paid ads. In a similar fashion, TV news coverage of a well-known author's appearance at your bookstore can only enhance the image of your business.

Two Good Publicity Methods

There are other ways to promote your enterprise as well. A camera shop can gain some community attention by sponsoring a photo contest. The prizes need not be elaborate—e.g., free rolls of film, free photo processing, or even just a small trophy or a blue ribbon. You might even be able to convince a wholesaler to donate a relatively inexpensive pocket camera as first prize. Once the local photo club hears about your contest, you'll probably find some new customers in your store. And if the local newspaper prints the winning photo from your contest—with your store's name mentioned prominently in the caption—so much the better.

If you operate a craft shop, you can quickly build a name for yourself by offering classes in your shop, promoted via flyers distributed throughout the neighborhood. The individuals who sign up for these classes will probably buy their materials in your store, and are likely to remain regular customers if they're pleased with what they've learned from you.

If you're entering into a unique type of business, you might think that no promotion at all is necessary. But even the most novel product or service will become tired after awhile, and any manner in which you can renew that interest should be utilized.

Henry B. opened up a poster photography business not long ago in a major shopping center in his community. Using a unique photographic system, he was able to produce a 20 × 24 inch poster of one or more persons in under two minutes. He began making huge amount of money immediately, with sales averaging well over $1000 a week—without spending a penny on advertising.

But Henry's profits began falling after his fourth month in business. As the novelty began to wear thin, he took action. He ran small ads in the local high school and college newspapers, feeling that his product appealed to a young audience. He also contacted a local TV station that often did human-interest stories on its nightly news show. A week later, a three-minute-long story was telecast about his business, and customers poured in once again. Henry learned his lesson about proper promotion, and has made use of it on a regular basis ever since.

KEEPING THE REGULAR CUSTOMERS SATISFIED

In the months and years after your business opens, you'll develop some regular customers. You'll probably eventually come to know many of them on a first-name basis, and you might even begin to take their patronage for granted.

But if your experience is like that of some other small businessmen, you'd be foolish to presume that a customer who comes into your store regularly will continue to do so indefinitely. Once you've gotten customers, you must work hard to keep them. Nothing could be more fatal than to become nonchalant about the clientele that you currently have.

The Value of "Extras"

Always have some "little extras" in your store to keep the regular customers coming back. A coffee machine, where patrons can help themselves to a free cup of coffee, can make your shop a more enjoyable place in which to shop. A restaurant that offers free homemade cookies at the cash register, or a bakery that gives away a cupcake or two to customers on their birthday, can bring those same patrons back into your store throughout the year.

You can also keep the customers coming back by stocking your store with items that you've found they want. Keep a close check on your inventory, and when you're running short on a popular item, re-order it. You can also drop a postcard to your regular customers, letting them know when you're having sales on items in which they might be interested.

Also, don't ignore service after purchase. Be conscientious about keeping the customers happy, even when you feel any complaints they might have are invalid. By making the exchanges willingly, you'll keep them as customers, which in the long run will more than make up for any inconvenience you may have at the moment.

"I've always operated my business with the old adage that the customer is always right," comments Dana W., who operates a drug store. "Of course, in reality, the customer is *not* always right. But I've built a reputation of running a store that accommodates my customers in every way. That's the only way I can compete with the chain drug stores in the city. People come to me because I make them happy. And by coming to me, they make *me* happy, too."

CHAPTER 12

The Ultimate Over-50
Success Tactics You Need

George H. is proud of what he has accomplished in his life. He now owns a successful glass and mirror company, but until he launched the firm in his middle years, he had to struggle more than most other people.

Since childhood, George has suffered from asthma, which curtailed his activity considerably while he was growing up in the East. He and his family finally moved to the Southwest, which allowed George a bit more mobility. But still, he has always had to cope with what is often a frustrating limitation.

Thus, when George decided to start his glass and mirror business, some of his relatives were skeptical. After all, they thought, George had never had a business of his own before, and the added pressures might be enough to make his asthma even worse.

But George has now ended the doubts about his capability of being a successful entrepreneur. Before he ever opened his business, he spent many weeks planning all the details of the enterprise carefully. He anticipated every possible eventuality, and he knew how he would react to any situation that might arise.

In effect, George took the pressure off of himself. He did not have to worry about any surprises. Through his own careful research and preparation, he was prepared for whatever would happen.

George has made that preparation pay off. He has parlayed it into the most successful glass and mirror company in his city. As well as the traditional products and services that his competitors also offer—like home and auto windows, mirror wardrobe doors, and storefront windows—George sells some very unique items, too, including glass tabletops cut to size, stained glass windows, church windows, and even custom-designed tiffany lamps.

By far, the turning point in George's business was when he received a contract from the local school board, which called upon him to install all the glass needed in the schools and administrative buildings. The contract, awarded for three years, has already been renewed once in George's name.

ACHIEVING THE "IMPOSSIBLE"

George H. has made himself an enormous success, although many people felt he had no realistic opportunity for prosperity. But George never let his supposed "handicap" become a burden. He planned everything so well that his illness had no significant effect on his business.

You can do the same thing. Everyone has insecurities when going into business for himself, based on either real or imagined obstacles. But no matter how imposing these obstacles seem, they can be overcome if you have the determination and confidence to do so. The small business community is quite competitive today, and the best way to prosper in it is to really *want* to.

10 BUSINESS DANGER SIGNS

Your will to succeed should not be so narrow-minded as to ignore any warning signs that your business is in trouble. In other words, don't be so overwhelmed with self-confidence that you won't allow yourself to find and alleviate problems before they develop into serious ones.

Keep your eyes and ears open, and some of the danger signs of a troubled business will be very obvious. Here are ten problems that should concern you whenever they arise:

1. Many customers leave your store without buying anything.
2. Many of your old customers have stopped coming back to your store.
3. Customers are returning a higher percentage of merchandise than you would consider normal.
4. Sales are down significantly over a comparable period last year.
5. You have trouble making ends meet from month to month.

6. Customers sometimes complain that your employees are indifferent to their buying problems.
7. Your best employees leave for jobs with your competitors.
8. Your merchandise is frequently damaged due to crowded displays and mishandling in your storeroom.
9. Credit customers fall behind in their payments.
10. The net worth of your business decreases.

Look over this list every month or two, and be willing to take some immediate action to correct the problems that exist. For instance, if your best employees are quitting, can you hold onto them by raising their salaries, or improving the benefits you are offering them? If merchandise is damaged frequently, can you rearrange floor displays to keep customers from bumping into them? If your profits are down from last year, should you launch an advertising campaign to bring people back into your store?

By all means, don't use a wait-and-see approach when any of these problems arise. If you don't try to alleviate a problem as soon as you become aware of it, you may find that you've waited *too* long by the time you finally try to tackle it. Once certain problems begin to gain momentum, they may snowball to a point when they are uncorrectable without a large investment of time and money. So take corrective action as early as possible.

WHAT CAN YOU DO ABOUT SECURITY?

One of the biggest (and newest) problems for small businessmen today is crime prevention. Of course, for as long as people have been in business, there have been burglaries, shoplifting, and employee theft. But until recent years, crime has never reached the crisis level we currently find it at.

Actually, small businesses are hurt more by criminal losses than are large ones. If you operate a small firm, your chances of being a victim of crime are 35 times higher than if you owned a large company. In fact, as many as 40 per cent of all small business failures can be blamed directly upon criminal losses.

No wonder, then, that you should be concerned about the security of your business. Don't allow yourself to become so involved with the day-to-day chores of running a business that you forget about the crime prevention aspects of your enterprise.

Of course, the best way of pinpointing crime problems is to hire a security consultant, who has enormous knowledge in this area and can advise you on the best prevention techniques to use. However, these consultants normally charge from $150 to $350 a day for their recommendations.

Until you can afford this professional service, heed the following suggestions, and you'll find that your store is probably as well protected as any in your community:

—Place locks on all doors and windows. Use locks that have a sturdy deadbolt and a pin tumbler cylinder. The bolt should be as long as possible so it cannot be released if someone tries to force the door open.

—Control the distribution of your keys carefully. If you are going to distribute some to your employees, give them only to your most trusted ones. It would also be wise to have each key stamped "Do not duplicate." If you're not aware of where your keys are at all times, you may just be wasting the money you've spent on sturdy locks.

—The windows in your store should be tempered or laminated, so as to be resistant to blows and breakages. Iron grilles which can be placed outside windows at night can also deter burglars.

—Bright lights, both inside and outside your store, can discourage burglaries very effectively.

—A watchdog that remains on your premises at night will keep any sensible person off your grounds. These highly-trained canines are normally leased, and they are expensive—$200 to $400 a month.

—Make cash deposits often to prevent large sums of money from accumulating in your store. Be as discreet as possible about your trips to the bank; take different routes and carry the money in an inconspicuous manner. Some store owners open their empty cash register drawers at night, to clearly show potential burglars that they have no money on the premises.

—An alarm system should be carefully selected. Shop around from company to company, comparing quality, features, service and price. Try not to buy more protection than you need.

—To discourage shoplifters, have your salespeople greet each customer with "Can I help you?" or "I'll be right with you," just to let them know that they are being watched.

—Your cashier should be very familiar with the price of all items in your store. A common technique of dishonest consumers is to switch pricetags, putting a $1.95 tag on a piece of merchandise that really costs $2.95. They'll purchase the item, but at the reduced price.

—In most states, you can retain a check verification service for about $10 to $15 a month. When you call the service, you will be told if a particular customer has a past record of passing bad checks. If he does, you should reject his check on that basis. These services also offer an insurance policy, by which you can insure checks of large amounts.

HELPING YOUR BUSINESS GROW

As the months and years pass, you'll become more and more experienced at making your business run smoothly. You'll learn more about your clientele, and what their buying desires and habits are.

"The best advice I can give any small businessman is to become part of the community," says Marvin F., who runs a hobby and craft shop. "If you can establish yourself as someone who gives something to the community, as well as someone who takes something from it, you'll be in a lot better position than if you only take.

"I donate a lot of hobby kits to hospitals, and youth and senior citizen centers. The local newspaper did a small article about my charitable activities one Christmas. The story did a lot for my image among all the people here. I also give the schools a discount when they buy materials from me. Every bit of good public relations helps."

In the same city, Marguerite J. runs a small hairdressing salon. She, too, has learned the benefits of giving something to the community. "Whenever the schools have plays or fashion shows, I contribute free hairdos to the girls participating," she comments. "My name is mentioned prominently in the program, and I'm always pleasantly surprised by the mothers who become regular customers of mine because I was willing to give their kids something without asking for anything in return."

Recently Marguerite made arrangements with a local TV personality to do her hair for free, in return for a mention in the credits of the talk show that the woman hosts. "It's the best free publicity I get," she says. "Every morning, my name is mentioned on TV. And don't think that doesn't help. Dozens of new customers have mentioned that they first heard of my shop on that TV program."

WHAT DO YOUR CUSTOMERS EXPECT?

Once you've established a good reputation in the community, do everything that you can to keep it. Let your customers know that you care about them as people, not just as consumers. Whenever possible, talk to them about things other than merchandise for sale in your store—e.g., discussions about their families, the local Christmas art show, etc.

It would also be wise to occasionally poll your customers as to what their opinions of your store are. Send them a postage-paid card, stating, "In order to serve you better in the future, I am interested in your opinions about my store. I would like you to answer as honestly as possible, since I am not asking you to sign your name on the card."

You can ask specific questions like "Were you served courteously?" or "Do you find the prices in my store competitive with others in town?" You should leave them space on the card to make comments of their own.

This survey will show the customer that you are interested in him and his thoughts, and you'll find that it will help build customer loyalty.

6 FINAL TIPS FOR SUCCESS

You've learned a lot in this book, and anything that could be said at this stage would probably be repetitious. However, there are some points that can be made in summary, which are so important that they could actually be said a hundred times without losing their value.

1. Plan ahead. Spend the time necessary to plan out your new business. In some cases, this may mean spending several

months getting everything ready for your grand opening. Nearly every successful small business has been well-planned.

2. Please your customers. Without them, your business won't be around for long. Give them a little extra in service and savings. If you treat them well, they'll be back again and again.

3. Create a positive image of your business. Newspaper ads and handbills can help build your clientele and create a good image for your company. Your firm will probably need constant promotion, and if used effectively, your business will boom.

4. Select your employees carefully. They will probably spend as much or more time with your customers as you. So choose them with care. Will they project the image you want them to? Do they already know something about the products they will be dealing with? Can they learn the workings of your business quickly?

5. Work for the highest possible profits. Keep your expenses under control, and keep your better-selling items in stock at all times.

6. Participate in civic activities. Take part in community events, and earn some positive publicity for your business. Never forget that your business is not located on an island; it (as well as you) are part of a larger community.

MAKING THE MOST OF YOURSELF

Once your business has been operating successfully for some time, you should give yourself a deserved pat on the back. You have overcome whatever handicaps you might have faced (i.e., age, finances, limited experience) and built an enterprise of your own. You've accomplished something which many people dream of, but only a relative few actually realize.

In effect, what you've done is to make the most of yourself. You haven't been content to make money for other people, but instead to earn it for yourself.

The value of this self-satisfaction can't really be measured. But ask any physician, and he'll tell you that contentment with oneself is as important a factor in your well-being as is good physical health, diet and exercise.

"I started my business at an age when most people are giving their first thought to retirement," comments Irving O., who runs a stationery store. "I'm so happy now that I don't think I'm ever going to retire.

"But if I do, I know that I'll look back on these times as the most rewarding years of my life. I guess you could just say that I'm very, very happy."

Index

C